Opportunity Denied

Opportunity Denied

LIMITING BLACK WOMEN TO DEVALUED WORK

ENOBONG HANNAH BRANCH

RUTGERS UNIVERSITY PRESS
New Brunswick, New Jersey, and London

LIBRARY OF CONGRESS CATALOGING-IN-PUBLICATION DATA

Branch, Enobong Hannah, 1983–

Opportunity denied : limiting Black women to devalued work / Enobong
Hannah Branch.
  p.   cm.
Includes bibliographical references and index.
ISBN 978–0–8135–5122–7 (hardcover : alk. paper) — ISBN 978–0–8135–
5123–4 (pbk. : alk. paper)
1. African American women—Employment—History. 2. Sex discrimination
against women—History. 3. Discrimination in employment—History. I. Title
HD6057.5.U5B73 2011
331.4089'96073—dc22

2010048424

A British Cataloging-in-Publication record for this book
is available from the British Library.

Visit our Web site: http://rutgerspress.rutgers.edu

Manufactured in the United States of America

For my daughter, Jocelyn

Contents

List of Figures ix

List of Tables xi

Acknowledgments xiii

Introduction 1

1. *Hierarchies of Preference at Work:* 8
   The Need for an Intersectional Approach

2. *As Good as Any Man: Black Women* 26
   in Farm Labor

3. *Excellent Servants: Domestic Service* 49
   as Black Women's Work

4. *Existing on the Industrial Fringe:* 71
   Black Women in the Factory

5. *Your Blues Ain't Nothing Like Mine: Race* 97
   and Gender as Keys to Occupational Opportunity

6. *The Illusion of Progress: Black Women's Work* 127
   in the Post–Civil Rights Era

Appendix 155

Notes 163

Index 183

FIGURES

1.1. Difference in the Occupational Income Scores of   16
Blacks and Whites in the North and South over Time

1.2. Difference in the Occupational Income Scores   18
of Women and Men in the North and South over Time

1.3. Difference in the Occupational Income Scores of Black   19
Women and White Men within Regions over Time

1.4. Occupational Income Scores of All Blacks, All Women,   20
and Black Women, United States, 1860–1960

2.1. Proportion of Black Women Workers Compared to   45
Proportion of All Workers Employed in Farm Labor,
1860–1960

3.1. Proportion of White Female, Black Female,   50
White Male, and Black Male Workers Employed
as Domestic Servants, 1860–1960

3.2. Proportion of Black Women Workers Employed   56
as Domestic Servants by U.S. Regions, 1860–1960

3.3. Proportion of Black, Native-Born, and Immigrant   58
White Women Workers Employed in Domestic
Service, 1860–1960

3.4. Detailed List of Expectations of a Domestic Servant   67
in the District of Columbia, 1939

4.1. Proportion of White Male, Black Male, White Female,   72
and Black Female Workers Employed as Craftsmen,
1860–1960

4.2. Proportion of White Male, Black Male, White Female,   73
and Black Female Workers Employed as Operatives,
1860–1960

4.3.   Proportion of White Male, Black Male, White Female,   74
       and Black Female Workers Employed as Laborers,
       1860–1960

5.1.   Proportion of White Male, Black Male, White Female,   108
       and Black Female Workers Employed as Clerical and Kindred
       Workers, 1860–1960

5.2.   Proportion of Black Women Workers Employed   111
       as Professionals, Managers, Clerical Workers,
       and Sales Workers, 1860–1960

5.3.   Proportion of White Women Workers Employed   112
       as Professionals, Managers, Clerical Workers,
       and Sales Workers, 1860–1960

5.4.   Proportion of White Male, Black Male, White Female,   114
       and Black Female Workers Employed in Poverty-Level
       Jobs, 1860–1960

5.5.   Ratio of Black to White Workers in Poverty-Level   116
       Jobs by Gender, 1860–1960

6.1.   Proportion of Black and White Women Workers   146
       in Clerical and Kindred Occupations, 1960–2008

6.2.   Percentage of Black and White Women Clerical   148
       and Kindred Workers Whose Incomes Fall at
       or below the Poverty Line, 1960–2008

6.3.   Distribution of Workers Employed in Nonhousehold   149
       Service by Race and Gender, 1960–2008

6.4.   Proportion of White Male, Black Male, White   150
       Female, and Black Female Workers in Nonhousehold
       Service Occupations Earning Incomes at or below
       the Poverty Line, 1960–2008

TABLES

5.1. Distribution of Men and Women Workers   100
by Occupation, 1900 and 1920 (by percent)

5.2. Distribution of White Men, Black Men,   101
White Women, and Black Women Workers
within Occupational Categories, 1900 (by percent)

5.3. Distribution of White Men, Black Men,   103
White Women, and Black Women within
Occupational Categories, 1920 (by percent)

5.4. Top Three Occupations by Proportion of White   104
Male, Black Male, White Female, and Black Female
Workers in Each Occupation, 1900 and 1920

5.5. Percentage Change in Distribution of Black Women   118
Workers across Occupational Categories, 1860–1960
(by percent)

6.1. Change in the Distribution of Black Women Workers   128
across Occupational Categories, 1960–1980
(by percent)

6.2. Change in the Ratio of Black Women to White Women   129
Employed in Each Occupational Category, 1960–1970

6.3. Change in the Ratio of Black Women to Black Men   130
Employed in Each Occupational Category, 1960–1970

6.4. Change in the Ratio of Black Women to White Men   131
Employed in Each Occupational Category, 1960–1970

A.1. Coefficients from Multilevel Analysis of the Influence   156
of Race and Gender on the Occupational Income Score

A.2. Distribution of Labor Force Participants by Race and   158
Gender (by percent) and Male-to-Female Ratio by Race,
1860–1960

A.3. Distribution of White Men, Black Men, White 159
Women, and Black Women across Occupational
Categories, 1960 (by percent)

A.4. Distribution of White Men, Black Men, White 160
Women, and Black Women across Occupational
Categories, 1970 (by percent)

A.5. Distribution of White Men, Black Men, White 161
Women, and Black Women across Occupational
Categories, 1980 (by percent)

A.6. Distribution of White Men, Black Men, White 162
Women, and Black Women across Occupational
Categories, 2008 (by percent)

ACKNOWLEDGMENTS

THANK YOU DOES NOT SEEM LIKE NEARLY ENOUGH to say to the many people and institutions that made this book possible. I owe a great debt to Hayward Derrick Horton, Karyn Loscocco, and Glenn Deane of the University at Albany–State University of New York for nurturing me and this project from its inception. Without you and your belief in me this book would not exist today. I would also like to thank Richard Lachmann, who read countless drafts and gave detailed comments that unearthed my intellectual blind spots. You helped me lay out aspects of my argument that I took for granted. I want to express my gratitude to Lindsay Hixson, Kecia Johnson, and Edelmira Reynoso, who were my cheerleaders, encouraging me to press on when I was exhausted and the story was hidden under mounds of data.

The sociology department at the University of Massachusetts–Amherst has been my intellectual home for the last three years, and I could not imagine a better context for pursuing this work. I am deeply indebted to Joya Misra and Donald Tomaskovic-Devey, both of whom read the entire manuscript several times, providing insightful comments, prodding questions, and encouraging words that infinitely improved the final version. My sincerest thanks to Melissa Wooten and Wenona Rymond-Richmond, who are much more than colleagues but dear friends, without whom I would have been unable to navigate the highs and lows of writing this book. For their invaluable research assistance, I thank Sharla Alegria, Jamilah Murrell, and Jonalis Carrasquillo. I also want to express my gratitude to the phenomenal staff of the sociology department, Wendy Wilde, Maureen Warner, and Juliet Carvajal, whose patience was never ending when called upon.

I am grateful to Adi Hovav and Rutgers University Press for seeing the promise this book held and helping me bring it to fruition. I am deeply indebted to the anonymous reviewer, whose critiques provided direction on how to highlight my primary argument with greater clarity and who was instrumental in reorganizing the book. I owe special thanks to Peter Mickulas, my editor, who tempered the business of completing the book with wit and humor. I would particularly like to extend my gratitude to Cecelia Cancellaro, founder of Idea Architects, for her editorial guidance and emotional support.

On a personal level, I would have been unable to complete this book if it were not for the assurance that my daughter was well taken care of while I plugged away. For that peace of mind I am deeply indebted to Joanne Faglar. Finally, I would like to thank my husband, Joel; my parents, Joseph and Mardette; my sisters, Rachel and Faith; and my daughter, Jocelyn, for believing in me and for the countless ways they made my life easier and created the time and space for me write.

Opportunity Denied

Introduction

FROM 1860 TO 1960, Black women's work and the experience of discrimination in seeking and keeping work was doggedly constant. The common phrase "you are what you do" was particularly true during this 100-year period when there was near-perfect matching of devalued jobs to devalued workers. Not only did Blacks and Whites, men and women, hold very different jobs, but the divide between the types of jobs they held was stark—clean or dirty, steady or inconsistent, skilled or unskilled. In this rigidly divided occupational landscape, the hierarchical dynamics of race and gender intersected to significantly limit labor opportunities for Black women.

Black women were restricted to devalued and dying occupations—farm labor, domestic service, and jobs on the industrial fringe—that other groups fled at the first opportunity. But Black women could not leave. During wartime or labor shortages they briefly gained access to more desirable opportunities, but they were repeatedly forced to reenter devalued occupations once these periods ended. It was not until the dual sources of their oppression, race and gender, were attacked by the Civil Rights Act of 1964 that Black women were able to participate on more equitable footing in the American labor market. Prior to this, the opportunity structure was closed and upward mobility was routinely denied.

Why does this matter? Why should we care? After all, progress has been made, discrimination is illegal, and Black women have increasingly gained access to more desirable occupational opportunities. The danger is that our failure to recognize the severity of the discrimination experienced by Black women historically leads to mistaken conclusions about the fate of Black women today. Contemporary discussions of the persistence of Black women in poverty, for instance, take place in the absence of any discussion of the historical context that the majority of Black women were restricted to poverty-level jobs until relatively recently. Despite the harsh realities of low-wage work—inherent instability and the limited opportunities for advancement over time—and the inability to make ends meet, many Black women today, as in the past, remain committed to the ideal of self-sufficiency in America.[1] It is not Black women's refusal to work but the lack of jobs that pay them a living wage that prevents them from rising above poverty.

In the contemporary era when meritocracy is valued (although rarely achieved) and group-based privilege is looked down upon, a historical assessment of privilege and disadvantage in the American labor market as it relates to race and gender is a worthwhile endeavor. It illuminates how maintaining privilege for some necessitated the subordination of others. The privilege of White men necessitated the subordination of Black men and White women. Black men and White women advanced only because Black women were left behind to anchor the bottom.

The uneven distribution of Black women across occupations remains an untold story. Scholars have tended to see the discrimination and labor restrictions that affected Black women as part of the larger experience of discrimination against all groups (with the notable exception of White men). The discrimination Black women experienced, however, was markedly different, even from that Black men and White women experienced. Although they shared Blackness with Black men and womanhood with White women, the possession of both Blackness and womanhood made the labor market a much more hostile environment for Black women than for either of these other groups. In the pre–Civil Rights Act occupational structure of the United States in which racial and gender discrimination was the norm, when Black men or White women took one step forward, Black women took two steps back.

Intersectional theory provides a lens through which we can understand the joint influence of race and gender on Black women's work. A singular focus on race or gender as the cause for the observed inequality among women or Blacks is insufficient since it fails to take into account intersecting systems of power and resultant oppressions.

A focus on racism and sexism is integral to understanding the past, present, and future position of Black women in America because the American opportunity structure does not exist in a vacuum. It is imbued with the biases and false perceptions prevalent within society at large, and the pervasiveness of bias leads to circumscribed opportunity structures for Black women. I argue that the occupational structure is a key location where racial and gender differences are transformed into class inequality. Black women's historically disadvantaged occupational position restricted them to devalued jobs that left them mired among the working poor.

By recounting this history, by emphasizing the powerful discrimination that emanates from the point at which race and gender intersect, and by addressing the progress of Black women in the post–Civil Rights Act era, this volume documents the historical evolution of Black women's work and exposes the socioeconomic structures that have located them in particular and devalued places in the U.S. labor market.

This book is organized thematically around the occupations to which Black women were restricted—farm labor, domestic service, and industrial fringe jobs. Using census data, I focus on the period from 1860 to 1960 in order to examine Black women's work when discrimination on the basis of race and gender was viewed as legitimate.[2] I chose to begin in 1860 rather than the post-emancipation date of 1870 in order to capture the work experiences of free Black women during slavery so I could show how the work experiences of free Black women shifted significantly after all Blacks were emancipated. I use qualitative sources drawn from archival documents and published historical accounts to contextualize the data and illustrate the ways that Black women were restricted to devalued work.

Chapter 1, "Hierarchies of Preference at Work: The Need for an Intersectional Approach," focuses on the need for an intersectional approach to study Black women's work. Race and gender are inexorably linked to occupational opportunity, and the consequences of placing Black women at the bottom of both of these hierarchies of power are dire. I demonstrate that being a Black woman in America prior to 1960 had a quantifiable negative impact on occupational opportunity above and beyond that of being either a woman or Black.

Although the conflation of race and gender characteristics and the associated challenges for Black women may be recognized, it is often assumed that only one is of central importance. This simplification subscribes to a form of sociological reductionism, where a complex set of observed facts tends to be explained only in terms of race or gender. By oversimplifying the cause of Black women's disadvantage, this approach may miss the actual mechanisms in operation.

In Chapter 2, "As Good as Any Man: Black Women in Farm Labor," I examine Black women's employment in farm labor from 1860 to 1930. Because slaves were brought to America to serve almost exclusively as farm laborers, a linkage between Black women's work and farm labor is obvious. After emancipation, many married Black women and their daughters chose to withdraw from farm labor. However, this experiment in self-determination was short lived as southern planters, aided by the Freedmen's Bureau, coerced many Black women to reenlist in the agricultural labor force because they were deemed critical to rebuilding the South. Outside of the South, strenuous farm labor was traditionally defined as men's work. The notions of true womanhood that surrounded White women painted them as frail creatures who were incapable of marshalling the strength required to tend crops. However, Black women's labor history as slaves first, freedwomen farm laborers later, and women never, justified their (often coerced) use in nontraditional occupational roles as needed.

Chapter 3, "Excellent Servants: Domestic Labor as Black Women's Work," explores Black women's employment in domestic service from 1860 to 1960. Interestingly, the rationale behind Black women's suitability for farm labor was that they were not considered women, but the concentration of Black women in domestic service was explicitly tied to the designation of household labor as "women's work." White women, both native- and foreign-born, dominated domestic service in the North and Midwest until 1900. However, native-born and immigrant White women's growing disdain for domestic service, greater occupational mobility, and increased educational opportunity after 1900 led to their departure from domestic service. Domestic service was dirty, onerous work from which White women sought to distance themselves. For Black women, however, it was the only occupation available to those fleeing rural plantations for urban life.

Chapter 4, "Existing on the Industrial Fringe: Black Women in the Factory," focuses on Black women's limitation to devalued jobs in the industrial context from 1920 to 1960. Although the majority of Black women remained in domestic service and farm labor, a substantial number were able to leave the farm and ultimately the household to enter more modern occupations, such as that of factory operative. When Black women were found in industrial jobs they performed the most undesirable work, often under hazardous conditions with no possibility of advancement. The condition for their incorporation into the factory was often complete separation from other groups, particularly White women, evidenced most clearly in the mandate for physical segregation. This separation provided the means to facilitate their unequal treatment, which included placing them in substandard facilities. And employers who were unable or, more often, unwilling to physically separate Black from white women used the absence of separate facilities as an excuse for not hiring Black women.

In Chapter 5, "Your Blues Ain't Nothing Like Mine: Race and Gender as Keys to Occupational Opportunity," I use the blues as a metaphor for the work experiences of Black women when compared to those of Black men, White women, and White men. From 1860 to 1960, the structure of occupational opportunities for U.S. workers evolved in significant ways. Farm labor and domestic service declined while substantial growth occurred in desirable occupations, such as the professions, management, government work, business ownership, clerical work, and sales. This growth particularly transformed White women's work, while Black men were increasingly represented in traditionally male occupations. In the context of the big picture of occupational expansion for White women and Black men, the routine exclusion of Black women from the new occupations is particularly notable. I explore how race and gender limited opportunities for Black women that were open to White women and Black men.

In Chapter 6, "The Illusion of Progress: Black Women's Work in the Post–Civil Rights Era," I show how dramatic the changes for Black women have been since 1960. Black women are often seen as the primary beneficiaries of the civil rights movement, and in fact they did experience the largest gains of any group in economic and occupational terms. However, concepts of gains and progress must be tempered by a historical understanding of the severity of their occupational restriction. A fourfold increase in Black women's wages by 1980 must be understood in the context of their artificially low wages in 1940 and 1960 because of their severe underrepresentation in desirable and lucrative jobs. Without this context, the so-called gains are inflated and provide a false sense of progress relative to that of other groups.

Additionally, Black women's economic progress was not sustained compared to that of other groups since it coincided with a period of national economic turmoil. Competition increased for jobs at the lower end of the spectrum as Black men lost ground in industrial occupations and the influx of new immigrant groups after 1965 increased the pool of low-wage labor that employers could draw upon. Industrial restructuring, the rise of multinational corporations and the movement of jobs overseas, and the transformation to a highly skilled service economy all acted to create new challenges that were not specific to race or gender but that disproportionately affected Black women because of their vulnerability in the U.S. economy.

BLACK WOMEN HAVE TRADITIONALLY OCCUPIED the bottom rung on the American economic ladder. Even today the general public interprets references to the underclass as referring particularly to Black women and their children. The "welfare queen," the false image perpetrated by Ronald Reagan and widely circulated in the popular media, is almost universally imagined to be Black, poor, lazy, undeserving, and in a cycle of poverty that is both intergenerational and her own fault.[3] This belief has led many to bypass an obvious yet often overlooked question: Why have Black women persistently been overrepresented among America's poor? Public opinion assumes the cause of Black women's poverty is their lack of self-responsibility.

But the truth is that employers discriminate against Black women in the labor force. They allege that Black women are unreliable and have inconsistent work habits because of the needs of their children. (Employers assume that all Black women seeking employment have children.)[4] Or they bemoan the attitudes of Black women, alleging that they do not have the soft skills such as personality, social graces, and friendly behavior, necessary in the contemporary workplace.[5] These allegations and misconceptions greet Black women seeking employment in low-wage jobs in America. The truth is that the vast majority of Black women work and have always worked. But many are still unable to escape the grip of poverty despite their adherence to a strong work ethic.

The pervasiveness of myth and folklore around the issue of poverty and the conflation of the nonworking and working poor in the media has obscured a conundrum: Why have Black women persistently been overrepresented among America's working poor? I contend that Black women's continued struggle to escape working poverty stems from their historically disadvantaged position in the American labor market. Relegated to dead-end, low-paying jobs and devalued solely because of who they are, Black women's employment options are extremely limited in a society that rewards Whiteness and manhood.

CHAPTER 1

Hierarchies of Preference at Work

THE NEED FOR AN
INTERSECTIONAL APPROACH

W.E.B. DU BOIS PROCLAIMED IN 1903 that "the problem of the Twentieth century is the problem of the color line."[1] While this statement was prescient, Du Bois failed to fully understand the problem facing Black women. Although race played a central role in limiting Black women's occupational opportunities, it was not the only source of their struggle. Mary Church Terrell's 1904 speech entitled "The Progress of Colored Women" aptly summarizes the challenges Black women faced: "Not only are colored women with ambition and aspiration handicapped on account of their sex, but they are almost everywhere baffled and mocked because of their race. Not only because they are women, but because they are colored women are discouragement and disappointment meeting them at every turn."[2]

James Baldwin reasoned that the role of Blacks in the U.S. status system was to mark the bottom, "so that White people would know where the bottom is, a fixed point in the system to which they could not sink."[3] Black women served a similar role in the U.S. occupational structure. They consistently held jobs that marked the bottom rung of the employment ladder. Employers almost universally saw Black women as secondary workers, or undesirable workers who were hired only as a last resort; this attitude ensured that they were perpetually underemployed or unemployed.

It is impossible to understand the near-universal restriction of Black women to devalued work without exploring the influence of both racism and sexism on which occupations were available to them. An approach that focuses only on race or only on gender as the reason for inequality among Black women fails to take into account intersecting systems of power. Privilege and disadvantage are closely linked to the complex hierarchy of domination and subordination that is created when race and gender intersect. This intersecting structure of power and oppression has had a distinct and documentable effect on Black women workers in America.

Relating to Privilege

Sociologist Cynthia Fuchs Epstein argues that "gender distinctions are basic to the order of all societies. Like age, gender orders society and is ordered by it."[4] Men and women are treated differently and do not have equal opportunities. Since the gender order is stratified with men holding the highest position, men have an interest in justifying and maintaining the status quo. The gendered division of labor preserves this hierarchy: the allocation of men and women to particular types of work becomes "a constraint on further practice," and the typing of women into feminized or feminizing occupations is used as an explanation for why women are not competent to enter other fields.[5] The devaluing of women's labor is a fundamental feature of the gendered social order. It has been accomplished in different ways over time, but it has always functioned to reserve high-paying and powerful jobs for men. Hence, gender inequality cannot be seen as being based solely in ideology; it is also based in the material benefits that men receive from their position in a gendered social order that systematically disadvantages women.

Men's power over women is linked to the gendered division of labor. Reproductive labor (primarily the unpaid work women do to maintain households and care for children) and productive labor (primarily the work men do outside the home, such as factory work and manual labor) are valued differently, leading to women's subordination. The distinction between unwaged and waged work leads to the economic exploitation of women as well. Women work at production and reproduction in the home, and when they work outside the home they often occupy low-paying jobs. The dual exploitation of women's labor—the facts that employers concentrate them in low-paying jobs and that they perform the brunt of unpaid labor in the home—is a fundamental feature of a gendered social structure.

Gender, however, is not the only basis for assigning reproductive labor to particular women. Differences between women belie the myth that women's experiences are universal. An exploration of the influences of race, class, and gender provides a much more realistic and complex view of women's subordination.[6] In the United States, reproductive labor for pay has traditionally been defined as the work of racial or ethnic women. During slavery and long afterward, Black women—in the South and later in the North—performed reproductive labor for White families; outside the South, other racial or ethnic groups and recent immigrants did this work.

The exploitation of Black women in the private sphere provided advantages for White women. With Black women cleaning, cooking, and doing child care, White women were freed from the burden of household tasks. Indeed, sociologist Evelyn Nakano Glenn notes, "instead of questioning the inequitable gender division of labor, [middle-class white women] sought to slough off the more burdensome tasks onto more oppressed groups of women."[7] The relational nature of race and gender has meant that at all times Black women have been defined in opposition to White women. The oppression of one (women of color) made the leisure and the labor market opportunities of the other (White women) possible.

Similarly, in the public sphere, race and gender led to the dual exploitation of Black women as workers. Conceptions of where Blacks and women belonged limited Black women to the most undesirable jobs. Consider, for instance, the task of washing clothes. Black washerwomen used to collect clothes and wash them in their homes. Before the advent of washing machines, the process of boiling water, scrubbing clothes, and pressing clothes with a hot iron was onerous. The rise of the commercial laundry in the early twentieth century gradually made this home-based business largely obsolete. Commercial laundries hired Black women in large numbers because White women largely avoided this work and Black men considered it women's work.[8] In firms that employed both Black and White women, Black women were limited to the "lowest paying, least-skilled jobs—hand ironing and flat work."[9]

This division by race was common in the workplace and provided the justification for the extraordinarily low wages employers paid Black women. Desperate to find work, they performed tasks no one else would do. There was no incentive to pay Black women a decent wage. Historian Jacqueline Jones depicts wage inequality in the middle of the twentieth century: "Nationally, women workers as a whole received less than two-thirds the pay of their male counterparts, but Black women took home yearly paychecks amounting to less than half of White women's."[10]

Employers did not view women as vital economic contributors to the household. It was common for employers to pay lower wages to women and pass them over for higher-paying positions because they were operating under the assumption that only men "needed" work and were financially responsible for families.[11] This conceptualization was applied to all women regardless of their marital or class status. Poor White and Black women workers were often not hired, and when these women did find employment, they were paid much less than men. However, the widespread assumption among employers that a woman worker had a man at home who was earning enough to support the household was not the case for most Black women workers, since most Black men did not earn enough to do this.

Black women and White women can be seen as fundamentally and distinctly oppressed groups, linked by their gender but separated by their race and their disparate access to power.[12] Failing to consider these differences and to interrogate their influence on the lived experiences of Black and White women leads to an oversimplified view of women collectively. As a 73-year-old Black woman observed: "My mother used to say that the Black women is the White man's mule and the White women is his dog. Now, she said that to say this: we do the heavy work and get beat whether we do it well or not. But the White women is closer to the master and he pats them on the head and lets them sleep in the house, but he ain't gon' treat neither one like he was dealing with a person."[13] Psychologist Aida Hurtado recounts this story to highlight the fundamental difference in the relationship of Black and White women to the privileged position of White men. White men seduce White women and reject Black women. But in a racist patriarchy, White men subordinate both.

While some scholars point to the universality of gender oppression as the basis for gender solidarity, Black feminist bell hooks reminds us that "white racial imperialism granted all white women, however victimized by sexist oppression they might be, the right to assume the role of oppressor in relationship to black women and black men."[14] Although the displays of privilege vary along class lines, all Whites have privilege based on race. White women cannot be viewed simplistically as victims of sexist oppression, for in doing so we perpetuate the invisible yet powerful privilege bestowed on them by their race. While gender oppression is universal, racism compounded Black women's oppression in order to distinguish and preserve a sacrosanct image of White women.

Contemporary Black feminist scholars have critiqued both feminist scholars and scholars of race and ethnicity for their inability thus far to address the intersection of race and gender as it pertains to women of color, and Black women in particular. In her seminal work *Black Feminist Thought*, sociologist Patricia Hill Collins critiques White feminist scholars for participating in ideological oppression by omitting the Black women's viewpoint. She also critiques Black scholarship and organizations for focusing on Black men and trivializing the ideas and experiences of Black women. In the scholarly literature gender tends to be treated as if it pertains only to White women and race tends to be treated as if it pertains only to Black men. Yet neither race nor gender on its own adequately reflects Black women's issues. Dichotomous thought—Black/White, male/female—does not include the experiences of Black women. Black women can be fully understood only at the intersection of both Blackness and womanhood.

Yet most scholars study either Blacks or women, restricting their analysis to Black men or White women, assuming that their experiences will apply to Black women as well. Or they lump Black men and Black women together, ignoring the ways that gender identity affords relative advantage and disadvantage in society. Quantitative studies often control for the influence of race or gender, but they rarely examine the interaction of both. Indeed, most scholarship conforms to the title of the book *All of the Women Are White, All Blacks Are Men, But Some of Us Are Brave*.[15]

Gender must be recognized as a system of power that accords privilege and disadvantage in conjunction with other systems of power, including race. This interlocking structure of power creates a complex hierarchy in which one group is dominant and all others are rank-ordered in relation to the dominant group. Sociologist Judith Lorber argues that although "men vary in power and privilege," men in each racial group "have a patriarchal dividend of power and privilege, compared to the women of that group."[16] However between racial groups, the patriarchal dividend is decidedly more complicated; White women are better off than some groups of men.[17] Class complicates this even further; lower-class Black men have very few privileges compared to their middle-class counterparts.

Although some scholars may abstractly recognize the conflation of race and gender hierarchies and the challenges this poses for Black women, many proceed as if only one is of central importance. Some scholars assume that if Black women had to pick their battles, they would choose to overcome either racial or gender oppression first.[18] This simplification subscribes to a form of reductionism that tends to explain a complex set of observed facts caused by an intermingling of race, gender, and other forms of oppression only in terms of race or gender. In oversimplifying the causes of Black women's disadvantage, such scholars may miss the actual mechanisms in operation.

Intersectional theory, in contrast begins with the understanding that "oppression cannot be reduced to one fundamental type, and that oppressions work together in producing injustice."[19] Therefore the focus shifts from identifying a single cause of oppression to discovering how multiple systems of oppressions are organized into a matrix of domination replete with "structural, disciplinary, hegemonic, and interpersonal domains of power" that structure the lives of those who exist on the margins.[20] A singular focus on gender as the basis for inequality among women, for instance, is insufficient because it fails to take into account intersecting systems of power such as race and class and the resultant oppressions this intersection creates.

For Black women there is no ranking of oppressions. The consequences of their placement at the very bottom of the power hierarchies of race and gender are dire. Although one category may have salience over another in certain situations, race, class, and gender structure all of their relationships and race, class, and gender oppression are experienced simultaneously, not just at the hands of men of all races but also at the hands of White women. Only an intersectional approach can give us an accurate picture of racialized and gendered experiences.

Is Black Women's Pre-1960 Labor Market Disadvantage Quantifiable?

Black women throughout U.S. history have remained in the lowest-paid and lowest-status occupations, despite historical improvements in the occupational status of both Black men and White women. Unlike Black men and White women, who each contended with only one subordinate status, Black women's subordinate statuses as both Blacks and women intersected. They were subjected to dual sources of oppression in a racist, patriarchal society that valued Whiteness and manhood.

The cause of Black women's labor market disadvantage is the subject of much debate. Sociologists Irene Browne and Joya Misra outline the core ideas. On the one hand, scholars argue that "social constructions of gender and race are systematically related to labor market dynamics to generate inequality."[21] Yet others argue that "even if race and gender are mutually constructed social categories, these categories have little influence on labor market outcomes in the long run."[22] I argue that the dissonance in these positions is attributable to the absence of a temporal distinction. It is clear that prior to 1960, race and gender were the primary causes of Black women's disadvantage. This fact must contextualize contemporary understandings and analyses of labor market differences that were shaped by a history of oppression.

Americans' unrelenting belief in meritocracy leads to a sanguine view of the role race and gender play in the labor market. We hold firm to the ideal that intellectual criteria, talent, and past achievements should be the only predictors of an individual's success. What many fail to consider is how the system has been rigged historically to preclude the success of minorities and women. The reality of widespread discrimination in the United States before the Civil Rights Act of 1964 inexorably linked race and gender to access to occupational opportunity and labor market success. We are barely one generation removed from a time when White-only signs were common throughout the South, and although segregation was informal and unwritten in law in the North, the rules there were widely known and rarely broken. The privilege of White men was clearly demonstrated throughout the labor market. Employers did hire White women and Black men for low-level jobs, but only when White men were not available or when jobs were clearly associated with race or gender. However, employers were universally contemptuous of Black women, and hired them only for the lowest-level and most onerous and disagreeable jobs.

Anecdotal evidence alone suggests that Black women were strictly limited to undesirable jobs prior to 1960. But is this difference quantifiable? Did it persist despite differences in the individual characteristics of workers? Other factors besides race or gender, such as whether individuals were married or single, childless or raising a family, young or old, literate or illiterate, or living in a rural or an urban area, had a definite impact on the job opportunities that were available to them. Did being a Black woman in the United States prior to 1960 have a negative impact on occupational opportunity after accounting for individual differences in marital status, number of children, age, literacy, and residency? To answer this question I used an objective measure of access to occupational opportunity called the occupational income score, a weighted average income of all jobs with occupational groups based on the groupings for the 1950 census.[23] The average occupational score was 23.9; the range was from 0 to 80.

Figures 1.1 through 1.4 represent the difference in the occupational income scores of two groups. If both groups were in similar jobs and received equal compensation, the difference in their occupational income scores would be 0. Blacks, women, and Black women all have lower occupational income scores than the Whites, men, and White men that they are being compared to, hence the negative occupational income scores for the first three groups. The figures visually represent how much of a difference there is in their respective occupational income scores. A higher negative occupational income score at the start of the period reflects a large difference between the two groups. If the difference between the two groups shrinks, the negative occupational income score declines. If the difference between the two groups grows, the negative occupational income score increases.

Figure 1.1 indicates that Blacks had significantly lower occupational income scores than Whites in all years in the period 1860 to 1960. The penalty for being Black was consistent across time. Although the relative size of the penalty varied by region, the general trend is strikingly consistent. The income inequality between Blacks and Whites greatly increased over time. Initially (from 1860 through 1880), the difference between the occupational income score of Blacks and Whites decreased, but they increased significantly through 1930 before undergoing a relatively small decline through 1950, thereafter remaining relatively stable.

The increasing gap in income from the turn of the century through 1930 is attributable to the movement of Whites into desirable occupations that were largely closed to Blacks. Because I am using census data, I am able to measure change only every ten years; hence the slight reduction in income differences between Blacks and Whites in 1940

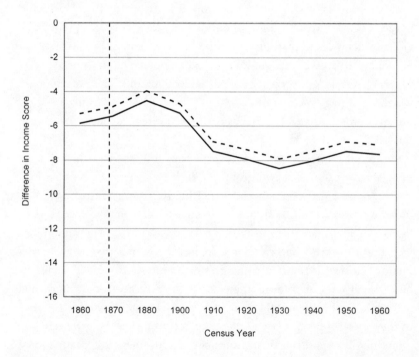

FIGURE I.I

Difference in the Occupational Income Scores of Blacks and Whites in the North and South over Time. This effect was calculated by summing the conditional effects present from the interaction of the Black, region, and time variables in Model 1 (see Table A.1).

SOURCE: Author's analysis of data from the Integrated Public Use Microdata Series, Version 5.0.

can be attributed to the federal New Deal–era programs, such as those administered by the Works Progress Administration, which extended new occupational opportunities to Blacks in the 1930s. Thereafter income inequality continued to decrease as the occupational structure changed.

The decline of farm labor began in 1920 and had culminated by 1950 as manufacturing, professional, and other desirable jobs increased rapidly during World War II and continued in the postwar boom. In addition, wartime labor shortages enabled Blacks to gain access to lucrative jobs that were traditionally closed to them, some of which they retained when the war ended. However, these changes in occupational opportunity only minutely changed the overall trend of economic inequality, which increased over time. All in all, Blacks and Whites were employed in different jobs throughout the century, and Black workers were crowded into lower-paying jobs.

Similarly, in Figure 1.2, the value of –8 for women in 1860 indicates that in that year, on average, women's occupational income scores were 8 points lower than that of men. The penalty for being a woman was consistent across time, and the general trend was strikingly consistent across regions. Unlike the trend for Black workers, though, the income inequality between men and women generally decreased over time, although it did not happen in a linear way. From 1860 to 1880, the difference between the occupational income scores of men and women decreased. It remained relatively constant through 1900, rose in 1910, decreased again in 1920, increased slightly in 1930, and then decreased in 1940. By 1960, income inequality between men and women was again on the rise, but it was substantially lower than it had been a century earlier.

The fact that the gap in income between men and women shrank intermittently is attributable to the fact that the movement of women into new occupational fields did not happen all at once. The decline of domestic service as a sector of the labor market, women's entry into and ultimate dominance of light manufacturing and clerical work, and the growth of women in almost every occupational category underlie the irregular pattern observed. However, equally central to this story is that differences among women are masked. Unlike the employment history of Blacks, for which a cohesive (albeit oversimplified) story

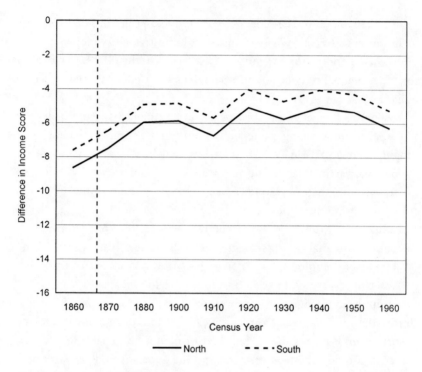

FIGURE 1.2

Difference in the Occupational Income Scores of Women and Men in the North and South over Time. This effect was calculated by summing the conditional effects present from the interaction of the women, region, and time variables in Model 2 (see Table A.1).

SOURCE: Author's analysis of data from the Integrated Public Use Microdata Series, Version 5.0.

emerges despite the collapsing of gender boundaries, the collapsing of racial distinctions complicates and blurs our understanding of changes among women over time.

Figure 1.3 indicates that Black women had significantly lower occupational income scores than White men in all years. Their dual minority statuses subjected them to discrimination in the labor force based on both gender and race. The penalty for being a Black woman was consistent across time and the general trend was consistent across the country, although the size of the penalty varied by region. However, the difference in occupational scores was substantially greater than the difference of Blacks' occupational income scores from those of Whites or the difference of women's occupational income scores from those of men. And unlike the pattern observed for women generally, Black women's income inequality did not decrease over time.

The extent of the differences when comparing Blacks to Whites, women to men, and Black women to White men is significant and clearly illustrates the importance of using an intersectional approach. As Figure 1.4 shows, in 1860, Black women had occupational income

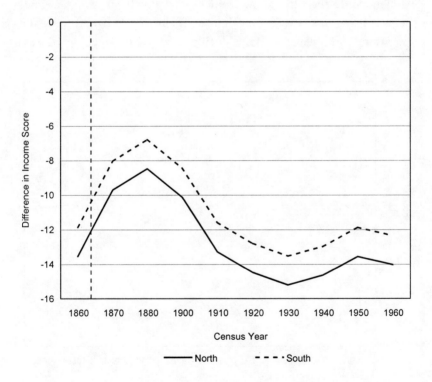

FIGURE 1.3

Difference in the Occupational Income Scores of Black Women and White Men within Regions over Time. This effect was calculated by summing the conditional effects present from the interaction of the Black, women, region, and time variables in Model 3 (see Table A.1).

SOURCE: Author's analysis of data from the Integrated Public Use Microdata Series, Version 5.0.

scores that were about 14 points lower than White men and this inequality was relatively unchanged 100 years later. The difference in income between Black women and White men in 1960 almost mirrors that of their counterparts a century earlier. If I had collapsed the data for women by race, that data would suggest that the penalty for being a woman decreased for all women over time. That would have grossly misrepresented the experience of Black women, whose penalty actually increased with time, although it fluctuated up and down.

Race and gender shaped the occupational placement of Black women. More than Blacks or women generally, Black women experienced severe restrictions that limited them to jobs where they did the same work they had done during slavery. The opening of new

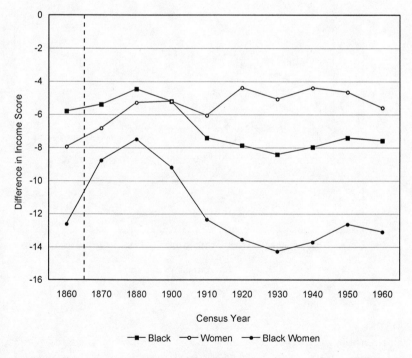

FIGURE 1.4
Occupational Income Scores of All Blacks, All Women, and Black Women, United States, 1860–1960

SOURCE: Author's analysis of data from the Integrated Public Use Microdata Series, Version 5.0.

jobs in the early to mid-twentieth century had little to no effect on their employment picture. Hence, income inequality for Black women deepened after Reconstruction ended, and it persisted through 1930. During this same period, income inequality abated for women in general. White women entered feminizing occupations that privileged Whiteness. Black men entered traditionally male occupations. Black women, however, stood outside the gates of occupational and economic change. They were neither White nor men. They lacked something that was essential in the pre-1960 labor market—a privileged status that would facilitate their uplift. Although widespread change in the labor market is evident over time, Black women were observers rather than active participants in this change.

A historical analysis of the labor force outcomes of Blacks that does not seriously interrogate gender is missing a crucial component. Similarly, an analysis of the labor force outcomes of women that does not seriously interrogate race is missing a crucial component. By failing to take gender and race into account simultaneously, researchers contribute to the erroneous belief that the labor market is neutral by gender and by race and suggest that Black women's occupational opportunities are restricted by their racial identity or their gender identity alone.[24] Nothing could be further from the truth. An analysis of the labor force outcomes of Black women must recognize that their experience in the labor market reflects "social constructions of gender that are racialized and social constructions of race that are gendered to create a particular experience."[25]

The intersection of race and gender shapes the life chances of Black women, particularly their experiences in the labor market, although scholars and pundits rarely acknowledge this fact when discussing their failure to find and keep work. The argument that race and gender are linked to privilege and disadvantage in the world of work challenges the uniquely American concept of self-determination; it points out that opportunity is given to some and withheld from others. This argument challenges the core of liberalism—the belief that equal opportunity is the hallmark of the U.S. labor market. The data shows that the history of the U.S. labor market is fundamentally the story of who people were rather than what they did.

The divergent labor histories of Black women, White women, and Black men bear witness to this fact. At the end of the nineteenth century, single and married Black women worked alongside Black men and White women in domestic service. For the most part, all three groups performed degrading work and were subject to the same poor working conditions and poor compensation. However, by the early twentieth century, both Black men and White women were able to leave domestic service and enter more desirable and lucrative occupations. The expansion of women's work into manufacturing, professional, trade, sales, and clerical occupations had little to no effect on the occupational opportunities of Black women. Similarly, the entry of Black men into industrial jobs as operators and craftsmen and into nonhousehold service jobs such as elevator operator and Pullman porter largely excluded Black women because these were viewed as male jobs.

The occupational advancement of Black men occurred because of male privilege, and the advancement of White women occurred because of White privilege. However, Black women had no point of privilege by which they could advance. Instead, their representation increased in devalued jobs, while the presence of Black men and White women in those same occupations was decreasing drastically. Black women were defined as menial, low-status workers suitable only for low-paying jobs that others shunned at all costs.

Black feminist Frances Beale argued in 1970 that the "racist, chauvinistic, and manipulative use of Black workers and women, especially Black women, has been a severe cancer on the American labor scene."[26] It is time for an integrative theory that examines the roles race and gender have played in the labor market disadvantage that confronts Black women. Race and gender are indicators of power within a hierarchical social structure. This power is relational—that is, it is premised on the idea that something (in this case, labor market opportunity) is available to one group because it is withheld from the other—and is maintained by simultaneous relationships of domination and subordination that reinforce the existing social order. The conflation of race and gender leads to a "continuum of dominance and subordination" that rank-orders individuals based on the possession of privileged and disadvantaged statuses.[27] This is exemplified most clearly within the realm of labor, where race and gender are keys to opportunity.

Indeed, in a racialized social system, where "economic, political, social, and ideological levels are partially structured" along racial lines, members of the race at the top of the hierarchy tend to hold the desirable jobs and receive the commensurate wages.[28] Further, they tend to control the ability to draw boundaries between themselves and members of other races, reserving privileged or desired spaces for themselves and restricting the access of others. As sociologist Robert Blauner argues, "One key to the systematic privilege that undergirds a racial capitalist society is the special advantage of the White population in the labor market."[29] Similarly, men historically maintained special privilege in the job market; society allowed them their first choice of jobs and they chose the most attractive ones available.[30] Women are defined as "secondary workers," relegated to jobs that are "typically at the bottom of the authority hierarchy, low in wages, dead-end and frequently insecure."[31]

The privilege of men and Whites in the labor market is self-sustaining, sociologist Stanley Lieberson argues, because "dominance will tend to perpetuate further dominance. This is because the dominant group—almost by definition—is likely to be employers, key co-workers, and form a specially important market, and their offspring will also be most suited and in the best position to obtain the most desirable jobs because their parents can invest more in their training."[32] Sociologist Charles Tilly explains it another way; members of the dominant group are able to hoard opportunity "by means of their power to include or exclude other members."[33] Queuing theory asserts that there is a hierarchy of opportunity as it relates to the distribution of social goods that follows from the various hierarchies present in a given society. Social scientist Lester Thurow argues that the labor market can be characterized as a labor queue, because "the best jobs go to the most preferred workers, and less attractive jobs go to workers lower in the labor queue; bottom-ranked workers may go jobless, and the worst jobs may be left unfilled."[34] I am using the concept of the labor queue as a metaphor to illustrate how racial and gender ideologies have resulted in opportunity-hoarding practices. Men and Whites have maintained their occupational privilege by perpetuating the labor queue and their privileged position within it.

Within the labor force, employers order workers according to their desirability and attractiveness into a labor queue. This ordering is not random but coincides with other structures in society including race and gender, which serve as proxies for desirability and attractiveness. Employers use these proxies when determining how occupational opportunity will be distributed. Although the centrality of race and gender bias today is highly debated, historically these attitudes created a consensus among employers about which workers they hired. White men, who were preferred workers along the race and gender hierarchies, were given the most desirable jobs; Black men and White women were given the less desirable jobs; and Black women were left with the most undesirable jobs or went jobless.

Movement along the labor queue was restricted. Upward mobility occurred when the size of the dominant group decreased or the number of desirable jobs increased, creating a shortage of preferred laborers. When there is a shortage of labor, employers must choose from the labor pool that is available. They are forced to consider groups of lower rank, in a stepwise process, first choosing from the second and third highest ranked groups (those with a single subordinate status—White women and Black men) and ultimately choosing from among those in the lowest-ranked group (those with dual subordinate statuses—Black women). Periods of labor shortage, then "can create a chain of opportunities for progressively lower groups in the labor queue," as sociologists Barbara Reskin and Patricia Roos argue.[35]

Yet the strength of employers' preferences was the ultimate determinant of whether race and gender served as a stepping-stone or an obstacle to advancement within the labor queue and in the occupational structure.[36] For employers with rigid preferences, group membership of potential employees was almost always the primary determinant of who they hired, whereas employers with more flexible preferences may have considered group membership insignificant, thereby affording Black women access to occupational opportunities that were traditionally closed to them.

Employers are not neutral actors; they make choices about workers based both on the desire for profit and the ideologies of race and gender. Although this belies some economists' assertions that it is against employers' interest to discriminate because it narrows the labor pool and increases the cost of labor, historically, employers acted on their racialized and gendered preferences and actively discriminated against Black women.

Economists William Darity and Patrick Mason note the pervasiveness of race- and gender-based discrimination in the U.S. labor market prior to the passage of the Civil Rights Act. Using help-wanted newspaper advertisements from the period 1945 to 1965, Darity and Mason illustrate that more often than not, employers preferred White applicants.[37] In addition, help-wanted ads listed jobs for men and women separately and drew on stereotypical gendered notions of labor. For example, men were solicited for managerial, sales, and labor-intensive jobs, whereas women were solicited for domestic service, clerical work, or waitressing. The degree of segregation by race and gender was clear in the advertisement for a switchboard operator posted by Nancy Lee's employment service, which requested that "all women applying be White."[38]

Despite these facts, many Americans are unwaveringly committed to the belief in the equality of opportunity. But equality of opportunity in America is an ideal, sociologist Peter Blau and Otis Duncan have concluded, "not an accomplished fact."[39] Occupational opportunities in U.S. society have always been circumscribed by the racialized and gendered attributes assigned to an individual at birth. Discrimination on the basis of race and gender was not a product of happenstance or irrationality. It was a deliberate act aimed at maintaining privilege for some, a process that necessitated that others be placed at a disadvantage. Hence, until the rise of the civil rights movement in the mid-1950s and the ultimate passage of the Civil Rights Act in 1964, which openly attacked the dual sources of Black women's oppression, Black women were stuck between a rock and a hard place.

CHAPTER 2

As Good as Any Man

BLACK WOMEN IN FARM LABOR

BECAUSE SLAVES were brought to America to serve almost exclusively as agricultural laborers, there is a clear link between Black women's work and farm labor. The use of Black women's labor during slavery laid the foundation for their exploitation long after abolition. In order to understand the labor market experience of Black women in the United States and the origins of privilege and disadvantage, we must begin with the initial work context for Blacks in America.

Blacks were not the only group to be enslaved in the United States. Whites held other Europeans, Native Americans, and Asians in servitude.[1] But the servitude of Blacks was significantly different from that experienced by any other group. Slavery produced an intergenerationally stable, coercible, racialized labor force. Black slaves were forced to perform backbreaking labor in the United States, but more than this they were objectified and dehumanized, a process that birthed a host of racist assumptions that were incorporated into the cultural construct of Blackness.

Legal scholar Adrienne Davis argues that the experience of enslavement was markedly different for Black women and Black men. First, the work enslaved Black men did was analogous to the work White men did on farms, except for the fact that their labor was coerced. While Black men were occasionally assigned women's work, Davis argues, "it was often for the specific purpose of humiliation or discipline."[2] However, Black women "performed the same work as men, while also doing the domestic work typically reserved for women, free

26

and enslaved."[3] The conception of women as the "weaker sex" did not apply to Black women. Indeed, Black women were not fully considered women at all. "In the eyes of colonial White Americans, only debased and degraded members of the female sex labored in the fields. And any White woman forced by circumstances to work in the field was regarded as unworthy of the title."[4]

Yet enslaved Black women could be found along with Black men "carting manure on their heads to the cotton fields where they spread it with their hands between the ridges in which cotton was planted." They "hoed and shoveled but they also cut down trees and drew wood."[5] Black women's compulsory performance of men's work in the fields appears odd in a society that crystallized gender roles, but their field work reinforced racial roles. White owners reconciled the oddity of Black women doing men's work using the belief that Blacks were racially Other. Thus, it was perfectly acceptable to compel enslaved Black women to labor with no regard for gender distinctions. Just as the Supreme Court decision in *Dred Scott v. Sandford* (1857) established that "the Black man has no rights that the White man is bound to respect," the fact that Black women were rendered genderless in the work they did suggests that they had no claim to womanhood that White men could not ignore.[6]

However, for Black women the experience of slavery went far beyond the indignity of being forced to perform "male" labor. The widely accepted notion of a Black woman as property and the children she produced as profit meant that slavery denied Black women control of their bodies. As Adrienne Davis points out, Black women's childbearing "created economic value independent of the physical, productive labor they performed. Southern legal rules harnessed Black reproductive capacity for market purposes, extracting from it the profits one might expect from a factory or livestock.... In its centrality to the political economy, enslaved women's reproduction was arguably the most valuable labor performed in the entire economy."[7]

The importance of Black women's productive and reproductive roles posed challenges for slave owners seeking to exploit both. Legal scholar Dorothy Roberts argues that the slaveholder aimed to accomplish two incompatible goals. He wanted to "maximize his immediate profits by extracting as much work as possible from his female slaves while at the same time protecting his long-term investment in the birth of a healthy child."[8] These goals were irreconcilable. "Pregnancy and infant care diminished time in the field or plantation house," yet "overwork hindered the chances of delivering a strong future workforce."[9]

The racial otherness of Black women made their enslavement, exploitation, and rape justifiable in the minds of owners because within the ideology of racism, their Blackness "made it psychologically easier to treat them with the brutality that the slave trade often necessitated."[10] Dissociating the concept of Black women from the concept of femininity furthered their exploitation; owners could view them as gendered or not in accordance with their wishes. When brute strength was required, Black women's status as slaves was paramount. The recognition by slave owners that "women can do plowing very well with the hoes and [are] equal to men at picking" led to the erasure of the gendered division of labor in the field.[11] Black women could be found "together with their fathers, husbands, brothers, and sons . . . toiling out of doors, often under a blazing sun," for up to fourteen hours a day. When their reproductive capacity was required, owners encouraged and even forced them to replenish the slave labor force, particularly after the overseas slave trade came to a legal end.[12] At all times, historian James Oliver Horton comments, they "were never too pregnant, too young, too frail, to be subject to the harsh demands of an insensitive owner."[13]

Over time, the association of "unfree labor with non-Western people of color" and "free labor with people of White European stock" became fixed.[14] "By the early seventeenth century, you had to be Black to be a slave in the American colonies," whereas before that time the term "slave" was more fluid in its racial association and could also refer to Native Americans and White indentured servants.[15]

The rise of democracy in the late eighteenth century and the associated belief that "all men are created equal" and "endowed with individual rights derived from nature and reason" was at odds "with lifetime servitude . . . unless Blacks . . . were to be considered less than human."[16] Certainly in practice Blacks were denied full humanity, and even under the law enslaved Blacks were considered only three-fifths of a person. But the widespread acceptance of egalitarian norms necessitated a justification for enslaving Blacks.

Racism, an ideology that justified the differential treatment of racially identifiable groups, was an outgrowth of the need to justify Black enslavement. To be sure, prior to this point, beliefs about Blacks' inferiority had developed, but historian George Frederickson argues that a full-scale ideological defense of Black slavery had not:

> In the United States racism as an ideology of inherent black inferiority emerged into the clear light of day in reaction to the rise of northern abolitionism in the 1830s—as a response to the radical demands for emancipation at a time when the federal government was committed to the protection of slavery. Defenders of black servitude needed a justification of the institution that was consistent with the decline of social deference and the extension of suffrage rights to white males, a democratization process that took place in the South as well as the North. They found it in theories that made white domination and black subservience seem natural and unavoidable.[17]

Indeed, in a speech before the U.S. Senate on March 4, 1858, James Henry Hammond, a Democrat from South Carolina, declared:

> In all social systems there must be a class to do the menial duties, to perform the drudgery of life. That is, a class requiring but a low order of intellect and but little skill. Its requisites are vigor, docility, fidelity. Such a class you must have, or you would not have that other class which leads progress, civilization, and refinement.... Fortunately for the South, she found a race adapted to that purpose to her hand. A race inferior to her own, but eminently qualified in temper, in vigor, in docility, in capacity to stand the climate, to answer all her purposes. We use them for our purpose, and call them slaves.... We do not think that Whites should be slaves either by law or necessity. Our slaves are Black, of another and inferior race. The status in which we have placed them is an elevation. They are elevated from the condition in which God first created them, by being made our slaves.[18]

The ultimate abolition of slavery did not fundamentally change the widespread belief that the subordination of Blacks was appropriate.

In fact, Abraham Lincoln explicitly stated his belief in the inherent inequality of Blacks. In a speech given at a debate in Charleston on September 18, 1858, Lincoln said, in response to a question asked of him earlier in the day about his belief in Black equality, "I will say then that I am not, nor ever have been, in favor of bringing about in any way the social and political equality of the White and Black races." He continued,

> That I am not, nor ever have been, in favor of making voters or jurors of Negroes, nor of qualifying them to hold office, nor to intermarry with white people; and I will say in addition to this that there is a physical difference between the white and black races which I believe will forever forbid the two races living together on terms of social and political equality. And inasmuch as they cannot so live, while they do remain together there must be the position of superior and inferior, and I as much as any other man am in favor of having the superior position assigned to the white race.[19]

The abolition of slavery freed Blacks from their designation as property, but they remained ideologically and, consequently, socially bound by conceptions of inferiority. Racism, once invoked, became valued in and of itself and it was an inescapable consequence that Whites would insist on maintaining a racist order predicated on denying the equality of Blacks. After the slaves were emancipated, there was no space for Blacks, the racialized Other, to coexist with Whites as equal citizens and competitors in the racialized social structure of the United States. Hence, the racialization of Blacks that was initially intended as a means to an end—justification for their enslavement—became an end unto itself, in that after the abolition of slavery, maintaining racial control and the racial privilege that it bestowed became the goal of whites.

In *Racial Oppression in America*, sociologist Robert Blauner argues that "labor and its exploitation must be viewed as the first cause of modern race relations."[20] Once the American labor system—which crystallized race and subservience as the appropriate role for Blacks—was established and "White supremacy and its packet of privilege became valued in themselves," it had to be maintained, and "people of color had to be controlled and dominated because they were Black,

Mexican, Indians, or natives—not only because they were convenient resources for exploitation."[21]

FREEDOM TO WORK

Emancipation presented a monumental challenge: How would Blacks be treated in a society that valued "free labor" but historically saw them as exempt from this ideal and fit for "unfree labor"? Would they be allowed to labor voluntarily and be accorded respect and civil treatment by their employers and society? Or would the duality of the U.S. labor system that was predicated on divisions between free and coerced labor, Black and White workers, reinvent itself?

After emancipation, the need for labor in the South was urgent. Many former slaves tested their freedom by leaving their owners. Historian Deborah Gray White notes that even before they were officially freed, slaves took advantage of the chaos of the Civil War and fled "whenever the opportunity arose . . . women less easily than men [due to children] but women whenever they could."[22]

Moving about freely was an exercise in the fruits of freedom; during slavery, the movement of Blacks had been closely monitored or prohibited altogether. However, "the extent of Black migration was negligible," historian Jacqueline Jones argues, since "most freed people remained concentrated in the Cotton Belt, in the vicinity of their enslavement."[23] Yet, even seemingly small movement was symbolic, especially for Black women, for whom slavery had been most restrictive. Consider a South Carolina woman "who left her position as a cook and traveled only a short distance to do the same work for a different White family, but now for wages."[24] Her former owner offered to pay double her wage, but she remained resolute, explaining, "I must go. . . . If I stay here I'll never know I am free."[25]

The desire to move was widespread, and many newly freed slaves moved to southern cities. However, U.S. Army officials took measures to restrict their movements. Historian Eric Foner writes, "In spring and early summer 1865, military commanders issued stringent orders aimed at stemming the influx of blacks into Southern cities."[26] In Virginia, for instance, General Ord "barred rural freedmen from seeking employment [in the city]. . . . In early June, soldiers and local Richmond police arrested several hundred blacks and shipped them to the countryside."[27] Southern planters were convinced that "only 'black laws' limiting [the freedmen's] freedom of movement would ensure a stable labor force."[28] Hence, for Blacks, the ability to move about freely was constrained by their obligation to perform specific kinds of work—plantation labor.

Black Codes, which were passed to specify the rights of former slaves, were often framed with the express goal of stabilizing and controlling Black labor. These restrictive codes illustrate the active role of the state in reestablishing the authority of planters over the former slaves. South Carolina's Black Codes, which were enacted in 1865, prohibited Blacks from employment in "any occupation other than farmer or servant except by paying an annual tax ranging from ten to one hundred dollars." The law further specified expected behavior: "labor from sunup to sundown and a ban on leaving the plantation."[29] Although some provisions of the law were modified in response to the objections of northerners, the spirit of the law remained and Black women were denied control of their labor in freedom just as they had been under slavery.

Historian Linda Kerber aptly notes that "the elimination of slavery as a form of work did not automatically eliminate an obligation to work."[30] Blacks who appeared idle were deemed vagrant and subject to compulsory labor. Black Codes passed in most southern states following the Civil War stipulated that "Negroes could be imprisoned for vagrancy and their labor bought by planters."[31] Eric Foner notes that "in Memphis, blacks were regularly rounded up in the fall of 1865 to meet the labor needs of the surrounding countryside" because General Davis Tillson believed that Blacks in the city were "lazy, worthless vagrants."[32] Although U.S. Army officials later stopped enforcing these laws, southerners replaced them with vagrancy laws, which served a similar function.

The Freedmen's Bureau, established in the summer and fall of 1865, was the institution charged with establishing a system of free labor in the South, but its ability to do so was severely hampered by an operating budget that was too small and its small size relative to the population of freedpeople it was to serve. Planters and freedpeople had very different ideas of the function of the new federal bureau. Planters saw it as a way of "putting freedmen back to work on plantations," while freedpeople looked to bureau officials as a bulwark in "prohibiting coercive labor discipline."[33] Both of these roles were part of the bureau's larger goal, which was to create a system in which "Blacks labored voluntarily, having internalized the values of the marketplace, while planters and civil authorities accorded them the rights and treatment enjoyed by Northern workers."[34]

This goal was at odds with the normative attitudes of southern planters and White southerners in general, who firmly believed that former slaves would not work unless coerced. Northerners who toured the South remarked that White southerners "do not know what free labor is." Southern planters replied that northerners "do not understand the character of the negro."[35] Many southerners believed that Blacks lacked self-discipline and would not work at all unless they were coerced. The belief that a worker would respond to economic incentives and other free labor principles "could never," planters insisted, "be applied to Blacks."[36]

The angst expressed by White southerners was triggered by the decline in Black labor, which had fallen by one-third, due, in large part, to the withdrawal of Black women and children from the fields.[37] Black men were partially responsible for this change; they were trying to protect their wives and daughters from exploitation in the fields and homes of other men. And Black women sought to leave the fields so that they could care for their own households and assume a more traditional woman's role. However, northerners and foreign visitors to the South who were advocates of free labor saw these efforts as a threat to the new labor system in the South.[38]

Outside the South, strenuous farm labor was traditionally defined as men's work. Indeed, in 1866 one Yankee journalist criticized a northern farmer and antislavery advocate who had women working in his fields: "An abolitionist making women work in the field, like beasts of burden—or men!"[39] A woman's work in a northern farming household of the early nineteenth century was limited to "dairying, from milking the cows to churning butter and making cheese" and "keeping chickens and gathering eggs."[40] Of course, this pattern pertains to a smaller-scale agricultural enterprise rather than to the large-scale single-crop plantations of the South, but the gendered associations about agricultural work still hold.

The notions of true womanhood that surrounded White women held that they were frail and thus incapable of marshalling the strength required to tend crops. However, White southern men were accustomed to using Black women as an agricultural labor force and had no qualms about hiring them to do such work after emancipation. In addition, for White southerners, Black women and domesticity were irreconcilable concepts. Black women's attempts to identify themselves as women and to restrict their labor activity to domestic roles in their own households were met with staunch resistance. The place of Black women, both northerners and southerners agreed, was at work in the fields. Black women who chose to labor for their families at home were chastised. A South Carolina Freedmen's Bureau agent, for instance, wrote disdainfully that "myriads of women who once earned their own living now have aspirations to be like white ladies, and, instead of using a hoe, pass the days in dawdling over their trivial housework, or gossiping among their neighbors."[41]

Southern planters objected vociferously to the decision of Black women to withdraw their labor from the agricultural sector in order to pursue domestic life. On the Watson plantation in late 1865, the freedwomen said they "never mean to do any more outdoor work[,] that white men support their wives, and they mean that their husbands shall support them."[42] Plantation owners lodged many complaints with the Freedmen's Bureau. "Maria," one plantation owner complained, "will not work at all." He added another complaint later that stated that "some of the women on the place are lazy and doing nothing but causing disturbance."[43]

The choice to remove women from the paid labor force was often a family decision. One female employer complained that "Pete is still in the notion of remaining but chooses to feed his wife out of his wages rather than to get her fed for her services."[44] Withdrawing from the fields was an option available only to married Black women and their daughters; single women and mothers were compelled to work out of necessity. But plantation owners were hesitant to allow women to "farm without a male partner." A Freedman's Bureau agent in Virginia reported that "there is little call for female help, and women with children are not desired."[45]

Planters and local officials used their powers of persuasion, and when that failed, they resorted to coercion to reenlist Black women in the agricultural labor force. Historian Deborah Gray White notes that "White southerners wanted them [black women] back in their fields and kitchens; they wanted their Jezebels and Mammies, and would beat, rape, and kill to have them back."[46] When Hagar Barnwell, a former slave, threatened to leave the plantation rather than work in her former master's kitchen, he took her "to a shed at pistol point and strung her up by her thumbs so that her feet barely touched the ground."[47] Whites often used violence and/or the threat of violence to compel Black women's labor in the postwar period.

When Black women did labor in the fields they were expected to pick as much cotton as men. There was no differentiation in responsibility by gender, and women who picked less than the quota were disciplined. Angeline Sealy, a Black field hand, was brought before a Freedmen's Bureau agent in Georgia on the charge that "she is very lazy and does not pick more than thirty to forty-five pounds of cotton per day."[48] The verdict in her case was "charge sustained—receives a lecture on her duties and is told that if she does not average from seventy-five to one hundred pounds of cotton per day that a deduction will be made from her wages." This was more than double what she had picked when she was able to set her own pace.[49]

During slavery it was common for planters to "learn" how much a new field hand could pick by whipping him or her to see how much cotton he or she picked when properly motivated. Once the individual's capability was known it became the standard by which their labor was measured. "If it [fell] short, it is considered evidence that he [had] been laggard, and a greater or less number of lashes [was] the penalty," and if it exceeded the original standard a new one was set.[50]

Although bureau officials did not sanction whipping, they did uphold the belief that Black women should be held to a standard of productivity that had been created by coercion during slavery. "Few Union officials," historian Jacqueline Jones notes, "were inclined to believe that freedwomen as a group should contribute anything less than their full muscle power to the rebuilding of the region's economic system."[51]

Plantations "historically required a disciplined, dependent labor force." However, when land or alternative sources of employment were open to former slaves, planters found it "nearly impossible to attract free laborers."[52] The difficulty planters encountered with controlling the free labor force led many to long "for the days when the lash could be freely used to compel slaves to labor."[53] When John Parrish, for instance, was left in charge of the Watson plantation in the spring of 1865, he wrote to the owner, who was away, exclaiming, "We are at the mercy of the Negroes." The former slaves had stopped working, rebelled against the overseer's authority, and "set up claims to the plantation and all on it."[54]

Planters soon surmised that the only way to ensure that Blacks labored in their plantation fields was to make sure they could not have access to land. According to historian Eric Foner, "Planters resolved never to rent or sell land to freedmen and condemned those landowners heedless enough of the broad interests of their class to do so."[55] They attempted to secure a submissive work force through detailed labor contracts that sought to formally reinstate the conditions previously specified by master-slave relationships.[56]

The former slaves on the Watson plantation, for instance, refused to sign a labor contract that would have effectively rendered them slaves by requiring that they obey "all orders from the manager . . . promptly and implicitly . . . under all circumstances," another that forbade them to leave the plantation "without written permission from the manager," and a third that charged the support of children too young for field labor against "the parents' interest in the crop and meat." This contract was rejected in "a loud voice and most defiant manner."[57] Not one former slave would agree to it. When the owner Watson returned to his plantation, he tried to reason with the former slaves, but his efforts were useless. He wrote, "They will suffer terribly this winter, but it seems clear that they cannot be awakened to their position and duties till they do suffer."[58]

Planters believed that their survival as a class depended upon one thing—their ability to command labor.[59] Indeed, Foner notes, "For those accustomed to the power of command, the normal give-and-take of employer and employee was difficult to accept. . . . Former slaveowners resented the very idea of having to negotiate with freedmen."[60] Former owners reacted with hysteria when freedpeople did things that were normal behavior for a free laborer in the North, such as leaving one job for a better opportunity at another. Planters resented the application of free labor norms to their dealings with former slaves.

In hindsight it is clear that the Freedmen's Bureau wholly under-estimated the depth of racism and exploitation that underpinned southern labor relations and the difficult, if not impossible, task it would be to convert the South to a system of free labor. Bureau officials thought, Foner writes, that "blacks and whites merely had to abandon attitudes toward labor, and toward each other, inherited from slavery, and the market would do the rest."[61] Free labor ideology rested on a core assumption "that all classes in a free labor society shared the same interests," but freedmen and planters both knew that in reality their interests were "irreconcilable."[62]

Further, the basis of free labor ideology was the belief in the exis-tence of opportunity for social mobility, "the ability to move from wage labor to independence through the acquisition of property."[63] Even Abraham Lincoln, whose belief in the inequality of Blacks and Whites was expressed above, said at the start of the Civil War, "There is not by necessity . . . any such thing as a free hired laborer being fixed into that condition for life."[64]

Freedmen's Bureau commissioner Oliver Otis Howard told former slaves, "You must begin at the bottom of the ladder and climb up."[65] However, most Whites did not share this goal, and a southern news-paper reported around the same time that "the true station of the Negro is that of a servant[;] the wants and state of our country demand that he should remain a servant." Or, as another put it, the "destiny of the negro race" was "in one sentence—subordination to the White race."[66]

Samuel Agnew, a Mississippi planter, noted that "our Negroes have a fall, a tall fall ahead of them, in my humble opinion. They will learn that freedom and independence are different things. A man may be free and yet not independent."[67] This view was so entrenched that a Kentucky newspaper declared that each freedman must learn "that he is free, but free only to labor."[68] Hence, in the minds of the planter class, freedom did not fundamentally change the status of Blacks; they were free in name only. Whites saw any attempts by Blacks to engage in self-definition or to taste the fruits of "true freedom" as indolence. Foner notes, "Charges of 'indolence' were often directed not against Blacks unwilling to work at all, but at those who preferred to labor for themselves. In a plantation society, a Black man seeking to work his way up the agricultural ladder to the status of self-sufficient farmer seemed not an admirable example of industriousness, but a demoralized freedman unwilling to work—work, that is, under white supervision on a plantation."[69]

Bureau commissioner Howard did not fundamentally disagree with southern planters; he believed that most former slaves would have to return to plantation labor out of necessity. But he disagreed with planters about the conditions of work for freedpeople. It was crucial, Howard believed, that former slaves labor "under conditions that allowed them the opportunity to work their way out of the wage-earning class."[70] The goal of Howard and many other Union officials was to redistribute confiscated and abandoned land to Blacks so they could labor freely and achieve independence. During the Civil War, Major General William T. Sherman issued Special Field Order, No. 15, which set aside land as a way of dealing with the thousands of former slaves who fled from their owners after Lincoln's Emancipation Proclamation. The order, dated January 16, 1865, said, "The islands from Charleston south, the abandoned rice-fields along the rivers for thirty miles back from the sea, and the country bordering the St. John's River, Florida, are reserved and set apart for the settlement of the negroes now made free by the acts of war and the [Emancipation] proclamation of the President of the United States. . . . Each family shall have a plot of not more than forty acres of tillable ground."[71] By the fall of 1865, the U.S. military had redistributed land to 40,000 freedmen. However, after President Lincoln was assassinated, the new president, Andrew Johnson, who disagreed with the goal of land redistribution and wanted to bring former Confederate states back into the Union as quickly as possible, "ordered the restoration to pardoned owners of all land except the small amount that had already been sold under court decree."[72] In late July 1865, Commissioner Howard "issued Circular 13, which instructed Bureau agents to 'set aside' forty-acre tracts for the freedmen as rapidly as possible," arguing that presidential pardons did not apply

to land that "had been settled by freedmen in accordance with the law
establishing the Bureau."[73] But President Johnson directed Howard to
rescind Circular 13 and to issue Circular 15 in September 1865, which
"ordered the restoration to pardoned owners of all land except the
small amount that had already been sold under court decree."[74]

By 1866, the Freedmen's Bureau had stopped promoting the idea
of Blacks independently working their land. Instead, it gave freedmen
the choice of agreeing to work for planters or being evicted from
property the bureau was reclaiming, per Circulation 15.[75] Some bureau
agents encouraged freedmen to sign unfair labor contracts, but many
of them equated these contracts with "a practical return to slavery."[76]
The contracts planters insisted upon put bureau officials in an irreconcilable dilemma. Although they believed that Blacks had the right
to bargain with employers as free laborers, the vagrancy laws that had
recently been passed meant that they were sometimes put in the position of threatening to arrest those who refused to sign a contract or
leave a plantation.[77]

Foner argues that the labor contract system fundamentally violated
the tenets of free labor, since the conditions under which Blacks
signed the contracts were coercive. Blacks "were denied access to land,
coerced by troops and Bureau agents if they refused to sign, and fined
or imprisoned if they struck for higher wages." It strains credulity to
argue that Blacks entered these unfair contracts with white plantation
owners voluntarily.[78]

Black woman's labor in the contract system also became a point
of contention, since under the system of coverture "the wife's legal
identity was subsumed under the husband's." This impacted labor
arrangements, as it was "wives' duty to provide labor" while their
husbands had "ownership of the fruits of that labor."[79] The Freedmen's
Bureau often required Black men to sign contracts for the labor of the
entire family, a practice that made men responsible for compelling the
labor of their wives. In Cuthbert, Georgia, for example, a Black man
was required to sign a contract that stated he would "work faithfully
and keep his wife in subjection" after she had "damned the Bureau,"
saying that "all the Bureaus out [there] can't make her work."[80]

Many men chose to explicitly exclude their wives from the labor
contract. In 1867, according to the *Southern Presbyterian Review*, "It

was a very general thing, last year[,] for the freedmen's wives not to
be included in the contracts for plantation labor."[81] Men preferred
that their wives engage in labor that benefited the family. In the Clark
family, Elias Clark labored under a contract, but his wife and children
worked only during the harvest. At other times, "they earned wages,
worked in the family crop, grew vegetables, took in laundry," and
engaged in other activities that benefited the family directly.[82]

Despite oppressive conditions, Blacks continued to strive for
autonomy; they were aided by the "labor shortage" following emancipation, which led some planters to be more flexible about contract
terms.[83] As Foner notes, "To attract laborers, many planters in 1866
and 1867 found it necessary to raise wages, promise additional pay for
harvest work, and offer land free of charge for garden plots."[84] Some
did far more than this. But the wages planters paid were not enough
to provide for adequate sustenance, much less facilitate social mobility
toward ownership of land. Additionally, successive crop failures in 1866
and 1867 undermined Blacks' bargaining power, depressed their wages,
and dashed their hopes of becoming independent farmers.[85]

Around this same time, the Freedmen's Bureau relinquished its
role as labor arbitrator and Blacks were left to advocate on their own
behalf. They resisted working in large gangs driven by White overseers,
as they had been forced to do during slavery. Initially, planters were
hesitant to allow Blacks control over their own labor, but by 1867 the
gang system had been largely replaced by smaller squads of Black men,
who generally organized themselves.[86]

It proved more difficult for white planters to compel Black
women to work for them. A survey of cotton planters after the
1867 and 1868 crop failure revealed the extent of planter anxiety
about freedwomen's withdrawal from paid labor:

> Planters in such places as Baldwin, Danbury, Muscogee, and Ogelt-
> horpe counties, Georgia; Forkland County, Alabama; Aiken County,
> South Carolina; and Panola County, Mississippi made similar obser-
> vations: "the women have quite retired"; "women seldom now work
> in the fields"; "all the women are out of the fields, doing nothing."
> "You will never see three million bales of cotton raised in the South
> again unless the labor system is improved," predicted a Georgian;

"one third of the hands are *women* who *now* do not work at all."
"Planters," another explained, "hiring twenty hands, have to support
on an average twenty-five to thirty negro women and children in
idleness, as the freedmen will not permit their wives and children to
work in the fields."[87]

As late as 1871, a South Carolina newspaper reported that the
absence of Black women's labor required a "radical change in the
management of [white] households as well as plantations."[88] A new
labor system was required that afforded Blacks autonomy while securing
the planters' interests. In theory, sharecropping accomplished this goal.
Landowners "provided land, seed, and other agricultural implements,"
while sharecroppers and their families "provided their labor for a small
"share" of the profits."[89]

For Blacks, sharecropping afforded a degree of autonomy in day-
to-day work. For planters, it solved the problem of procuring laborers
because workers had an interest in maximizing the crop and remaining
on the land until it had been harvested. Although sharecropping began
as a compromise between Blacks and planters about how labor would
be organized (in the family unit) and wages would be paid (as a share
of the crop), the new system unofficially reestablished the authority of
the planter because the sharecropper was once again tethered to the
planter's land.

Further, the debilitating credit system left the average Black
family in a "cycle of debt to landowners and merchants who had
advanced food, supplies, and equipment for a share of the family's meager crop."[90] Black families often mobilized women's labor
to reduce their dependence on the credit system by producing food or
performing domestic tasks for income. Anderson Scales, for instance,
"counted on his wife's work for the family . . . fertilizing soil, tending
a vegetable garden and fruit trees, and taking in washing."[91]

However, some plantation owners "discouraged or flatly forbade
tenants from keeping a garden or raising hogs so as to force them to be
completely dependent on the commissary."[92] Some required that "all
land rented to croppers had to be devoted to cash crops (cotton)."[93]
These actions had the dual effect of ensuring Blacks' dependence on
the credit system, which charged up to 25 percent interest on supplies

purchased on credit, and requiring the labor of women and children to maximize the crop.

Sharecropping soon became a form of "debt bondage," since at the end of the year when it was time to settle debts, Blacks frequently owed planters much more than their share of the crop was worth. They were then required to remain on the plantation until their debt was paid in full, although it was likely that the next year would find them in a similar position. States were often complicit in this coercive system, as illustrated by a Georgia law that allowed sharecroppers and others "who attempted to quit while owing money to the employer to be charged with fraudulently procuring money and sentenced to prison or forced to work."[94]

Freedom for Blacks, then, was fleeting. Coercive labor systems quickly reestablished old patterns that characterized Blacks' employment in farm labor for decades afterward. Historian Jacqueline Jones argues that freedom can be measured by the degree of control an individual has over his or her labor and family life. By both measures Black freedom existed in word only.[95] Further, sociologist Evelyn Nakano Glenn argues that "although they were legally free, they lacked a material base for true independence."[96] More often than not Black men and women worked for their former slave owners, who sought to manage a relationship that was by definition exploitive.

BLACK WOMEN IN FARM LABOR, 1860–1960

A more precise examination of Black women's engagement in farm labor is needed to demonstrate the extent to which their occupational choices were restricted after the initial period of Reconstruction, but first it is necessary to clearly define farm labor. Farm labor includes all types of agricultural laborers—sharecroppers, tenant farmers, seasonal laborers, and farm owners—since it is not possible to accurately distinguish between these groups in census data over time.

Agricultural labor falls into two broad occupational categories in the census. First is the category of farmers, which is subdivided into farmers (owners and tenants) and farm managers. The second category, farm laborers, is subdivided into farm foremen, farm laborers who were wage workers, farm laborers who were unpaid family workers, and farm service laborers who were self-employed. Many distinctions are lost in this categorization, including the important distinction between farm owner and sharecropper. For example, in 1870, census takers were required to ask for the "profession[,] occupation, or trade" of each member of a household.[97] Sharecroppers were technically farmers and were counted as such by census takers, although the organization and execution of their labor more closely approximates that of a farm laborer.

To call sharecroppers farmers is misleading at best and inaccurate at worst, since the title of farmer implies control and/or ownership of land, which very few sharecroppers had. Instead, many were subject to close supervision by "riders" employed by landowners "who traveled from farm to farm monitoring tenants," meting out punishment at will.[98] "Early twentieth-century Cotton Belt plantations," Glenn argues, "more closely resembled industrial establishments than conglomerations of family farms."[99]

Further, the representation of men and women as farmers and farm laborers in the U.S. census has been problematized due to the pervasiveness of gender bias.[100] It was not uncommon for the census enumerator to assign work roles and status by gender, denoting men as farmers and women as farm laborers regardless of their actual labor roles. In order to remedy this problem, I have chosen to collapse these two occupational categories, farmer and farm labor, into one category called farm labor.

Since my focus is on the type of work Black women did in broad strokes, erasing this distinction does not hinder my analysis. Indeed, the various titles applied to sharecroppers, tenants, and seasonal laborers do not reflect differences in these workers' experience of their work. Although it is true that these groups had varying control over the organization of their work, all were subject to a landowner, and the exacting demands of farm labor were universal.

From sunup to sundown, farm laborers could be found in the field performing hard, backbreaking work. Emancipation freed Blacks from their designation as slaves and from constant surveillance and punishment from the overseer, but the work of picking cotton, for instance, an activity that many Black women did, remained a dirty, grueling job. "Hoe Emma Hoe," a call-and-response work song from slavery times, describes the tasks of a Black woman in the field.[101]

CALLER: Hoe Emma Hoe, you turn around dig a hole in the
    ground, Hoe Emma Hoe.
CHORUS: Hoe Emma Hoe, you turn around dig a hole in the
    ground, Hoe Emma Hoe.
CALLER: Emma, you from the country.
CHORUS: Hoe Emma Hoe, you turn around dig a hole in the
    ground, Hoe Emma Hoe.
CALLER: Emma help me to pull these weeds.
CHORUS: Hoe Emma Hoe, you turn around dig a hole in the
    ground, Hoe Emma Hoe.
CALLER: Emma work harder than two grown men.
CHORUS: Hoe Emma Hoe, you turn around dig a hole in the
    ground, Hoe Emma Hoe.
(Repeat)

The emphasis of the caller on the fact that "Emma work harder than two grown men" highlights slaves' perception of the standards to which women were held and the ability of Black women to meet those standards. Women were to be as strong as or stronger than men because men's labor on the farm was seen as the standard of success. Farm labor was men's work; to do this work well meant the women had to be as good as men. Black women were able to do men's work and do it well.

The importance of region in Black women's employment in farm labor cannot be overstated. It was a distinctly southern phenomenon. Prior to emancipation, roughly 60 percent of free Black women farm laborers were found in the South. After emancipation, close to 90 percent were found in the South. This pattern persisted for decades; in 1960, nearly 75 percent of Black women farm laborers were in the South, although their numbers in the West and Midwest were growing.

This, of course, had everything to do with the concentration of Blacks in the South over this period. In 1860, less than 60 percent of free Black women were in the South. After emancipation through the start of the Great Migration in 1910, nearly 90 percent of Black women were found in the South, and at the end of the nineteenth century the majority of the Black population in the South was still concentrated in rural areas. Farm labor was all that they were able to do; domestic service was largely an urban phenomenon. By 1930, the effect of the Great Migration is clear; the percentage of Black women in the South had dropped substantially to about 75 percent. In addition, many Black women on their way to the North, Midwest, and West moved out of rural areas and into cities, further diminishing the size of the rural workforce and the number of Black women engaged in farm labor.

However, increasing mechanization from the late nineteenth century onward reduced the centrality of manual labor to agricultural production, and farm labor receded to the periphery of the labor market. In 1860, farm labor was the largest employment sector in

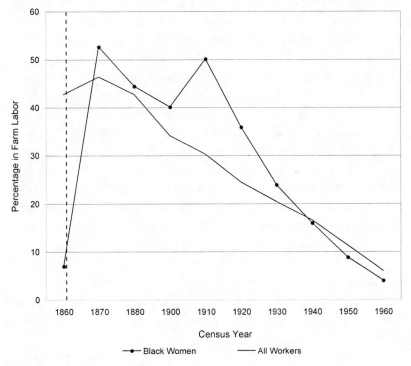

FIGURE 2.1

Proportion of Black Women Workers Compared to Proportion of All Workers Employed in Farm Labor, 1860–1960

SOURCE: Author's analysis of data from the Integrated Public Use Microdata Series, Version 5.0.

the labor force, employing 43 percent of all workers. By 1900, only about one-third of workers remained in farm labor, and that statistic continued to decline throughout the twentieth century. Black women's engagement in farm labor, however, tells a slightly different tale. For the majority of the period, 1870 to 1940, the proportion of Black women exceeded the proportion of all workers engaged in farm labor. Although Black women represented less than 5 percent of the nation's labor force, they were concentrated in this employment sector, which represented dirty and arduous work, and they remained in this sector as it declined.

Just before emancipation, very few free Black women, about 7 percent, were engaged in farm labor. This stands in sharp contrast to their employment picture after 1870 (the year that emancipated Blacks were included in census counts for the first time), when the majority of free Black women, nearly 53 percent, were engaged in farm labor. Census data is taken every ten years, so we are not able to capture the labor patterns immediately after emancipation, but the historical record suggests (as described above) that a significant proportion of Black women chose to withdraw from the agricultural labor force. Estimates by economic historians confirm that "by the 1870s the amount of Black labor in the fields had dropped to one-quarter or one-third pre-emancipation levels."[102]

From 1870 through 1920, roughly 40 to 50 percent of all employed Black women were in farm labor. After 1920, Black women's engagement in farm labor decreased from 24 percent in 1930 to 15 percent in 1940, although on the cotton plantations of the Depression-era South, they could be found everywhere. "A stooped woman dragging a heavy cotton sack. Usually she wears a slatted sunbonnet, and her arms and neck are swathed with rags to protect them from the blistering heat. This is the woman," journalist Elaine Ellis remarks, "who civilization passed by."[103]

By 1950, less than 10 percent of Black women were engaged in farm labor. Historian Jacqueline Jones notes that "the most striking change in patterns of Black women's work during the century after slavery resulted from the contraction in the agricultural sector of the economy."[104] This decline was due to several changes, including the movement of Blacks from rural areas to urban centers, the increasing mechanization of agricultural labor, and the industrialization of the South. But most important, the decline in Black women's participation in agricultural work was about increasing opportunities for them in other dirty and otherwise disagreeable occupations, especially domestic service.

BLACK WOMEN IN THE UNITED STATES have been defined by others, often vilified, and almost always exploited. During slavery, they held the dual status of person and property under the three-fifths compromise, but the interpretation of the law often reinforced the notion that they were "more property than person."[105] They were valued as laborers and as reproductive bodies, but they were never acknowledged as women. Slavery laid the groundwork for the exploitation of Black women in the U.S. labor force, since they were the only labor group for whom gender roles were inconsequential.

Slavery highlighted the fundamental distinction between forced and free labor. In the United States, this was an innately racialized difference. Yet as this distinction slowly eroded after emancipation a new and insidious plan was hatched to distinguish and ultimately justify the preservation of privileged labor market positions for Whites. During slavery, Whites associated degrading labor with the *slave status* of the laborer; after slavery, they associated such labor with the *race* of the worker. In other words, before emancipation, degrading work was reserved for slaves. After emancipation, it was reserved for Blacks. Once this labor pattern was reestablished during Reconstruction it defined Black labor for decades afterward. Blacks were expected to labor in the fields not because they were slaves but because they were Black.

The paradox of Black women's relationship to femininity—the fact that they are biologically female but were excluded from society's definition of the category "women"—was not resolved with emancipation. Rather, this paradox is illustrated clearly in the two occupations they came to dominate immediately before and long after emancipation—farm labor and domestic service. Indeed, the fluidity with which Black women's identity as women was recognized or disregarded would be key to their exploitation as laborers for years to come.

It was a curious paradox. At the same time that White women were being encouraged to attend to hearth and home, Black women were scorned for "being out of the field doing nothing," "playing the lady," and succumbing to the "evil of female loaferism."[106] But planters' frantic disapproval of the decision of Black women to withdraw from the labor force after emancipation went far beyond a war of words, and planters were unrelenting in their quest for absolute control of Black women's labor.

More sinister than individual planters' use of violence and the threat of violence to coerce labor was the active role southern states played in reinstituting slavery by another name via Black Codes and vagrancy laws. Vagrancy laws stipulated that "officials could apprehend an 'idler' who had no visible means of subsistence and then hire him or her out at the available wage rate, usually as a servant or common laborer."[107] Although these laws were race-neutral, "Blacks were overwhelmingly those arrested and ordered to work."[108] Vagrancy laws were a mechanism Whites used to reestablish a system of coercible labor for Blacks in the South. The new system of sharecropping, which at one time offered the promise of familial protection and autonomy for Black women, became a coercive institution that prohibited any semblance of independent family farming. Ultimately, Black women's attempt to identify with the ideals of womanhood and put the cares and desires of their families above that of the market by withdrawing from the labor force was short lived. This was permitted expression only within their homes, and only to the extent that their efforts to benefit their households and families did not take away from their labor in the field.

CHAPTER 3

Excellent Servants

DOMESTIC SERVICE
AS BLACK WOMEN'S WORK

WHILE BLACK WOMEN were deemed suitable for farm labor because they were not considered real women, their concentration in domestic service was explicitly tied to the designation of household labor as the work of racial or ethnic women. The assumption that this linkage arose during slavery when Black women served in gender-normative roles as house slaves—tending to children, cooking meals, and doing laundry—is incorrect. Although many Black women served as house slaves, 85 percent of enslaved Black women worked in the fields.[1]

An entirely different pattern emerged among free Black women. In 1860, nearly 70 percent were employed as domestic servants. During the same period, almost half of all employed White women were also domestic workers, since it was one of the few occupational options available to women. White domestic workers were primarily employed outside the South, while Black women were primarily employed within the South. Men, both Black and White, entered domestic service only when there were no alternatives, and the proportion of men in domestic service was extraordinarily low compared to that of women.[2] Of all free Black men, only about 4 percent were employed as domestic servants in 1860, a statistic that remained relatively static through 1960. Similarly, less than 1 percent of employed White men were ever in domestic service. Although domestic service represented a very small percentage of all occupations (about 8 percent in 1860), it largely defined Black women's work for the course of a century.

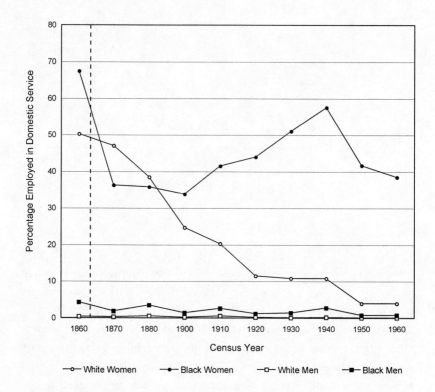

FIGURE 3.1

Proportion of White Female, Black Female, White Male, and Black Male Workers Employed as Domestic Servants, 1860–1960

SOURCE: Author's analysis of data from the Integrated Public Use Microdata Series, Version 5.0

In 1870, after emancipation, the census data shows a departure from the occupational pattern observed in 1860 for free Black women. This is because formerly enslaved Black women were included as paid laborers for the first time in the U.S. census. (Slaves were counted in the 1860 census only for the purposes of taxing owners and allocating political representation to southern states; each adult slave counted as three-fifths of a person.) The 1870 census shows that at the national level, the majority of Black women remained engaged in the work that most of them had done as slaves—farm labor. Only in the South did Black women constitute a significant contingent of domestic workers, since most White women in that region refused to enter the occupation because of its association with Black women under slavery. Yet the demand for Black women's labor in the fields was so great that until farming experienced widespread decline in the 1920s, it dominated their labor in the South.

Although both Black and White women performed domestic service, White women resisted the label "servant." In fact, most American workers who performed servile tasks resisted that term, preferring "help," "hired help," or "hired man, woman, or girl."[3] Consider the following conversation, in 1807, between an English visitor to a northern U.S. city and the female domestic worker who answered the door: "Is your master at home? . . . I have no master. . . . Don't you live here? . . . I stay here. . . . And who are you then? . . . Why I am Mr.—'s help. I'd have you to know, man, that I am no sarvant; none but negers are servants."[4] By the mid-nineteenth century this sentiment was unchanged. A British traveler, Charles Mackay, who visited the United States between 1857 and 1858 observed:

> As is well known, a domestic servant of American birth, and without Negro blood in his or her veins, who condescends to help the mistress or master of a household in making the beds, milking the cows, cooking the dinner, grooming the horse, or driving the carriage, is not a servant, but a "help." "Help wanted," is the common heading of advertisement in the North, where servants are required. A native American of Anglo-Saxon lineage thinks himself born to lead and to rule, and scorns to be considered a "servant," or even to tolerate the name. . . . But the negro is not a help; he is emphatically a servant.[5]

It is clear that from the early years of the nineteenth century, the prevailing notion was that only Blacks were fit to be servants, even though Black and White domestic workers did virtually the same work. While white domestic workers often appeared fluid and informal compared to the rigidity of the servant role, the only real difference between the two groups was the formal title of servant. White domestic workers objected to, and were often able to avoid, the designation of servant, while Black domestic workers had no say in how their work role was named.

Another difference was the hiring practices that were used for each group. The hiring of domestic workers was often highly personalized. In rural areas in the North, notes historian Faye Dudden, "few women participated in wage labor, and there was no formal group of wage workers called domestic servants, only neighbor girls known by name."[6] This degree of familiarity with domestic workers (and their families) promoted mutual respect and served as a form of protection for the women, preventing unjust treatment by employers. No such familiarity or protection existed for Black domestic workers. The race of domestic workers also often implied length of tenure in the occupation. White workers were seen as engaging in a transient arrangement, whereas Black servants were expected to occupy the role indefinitely. Free Blacks technically had a choice as to whether or not they would remain a servant in a particular household, but abject poverty and few occupational alternatives prohibited any real movement.[7]

Ultimately, the experience of Black women and other racial or ethnic minorities in domestic service was largely defined by their racial dissimilarity from their employers. Sociologist Evelyn Nakano Glenn argues that the ideology of the dominant group defined "the proper place of these groups as in service: they belonged there, just as it was the dominant group's place to be served."[8] Significantly, these ideas took hold before Black women dominated domestic service. In 1850, for instance, 80 percent of domestic servants in New York City were Irish women and there was a growing use of Irish labor.[9] Although free Black women made up a minority of workers in the North, the notion that Black women were mostly servants was widespread.

Eventually, domestic service became defined in occupational terms that were more rigid than the informality of the neighborhood arrangement of the rural North in the early nineteenth century. Formal titles were instituted that determine the type of work performed. A *New York Times* article on domestic servants published on July 7, 1872, outlined three major divisions of female domestic servants: "cooks," "upstairs girls," and girls for "general house-work." The expectations of each role were somewhat fixed by the time this article was written. "The 'cooks' do what their name implies and the washing, too; while the 'upstairs' girls' sweep, wait on the door and table, 'setting' the latter, and during spare time 'make' the beds and 'keep' the children. The 'girl for general house-work' is a comprehensive creature, who engages to do all of the foregoing 'for a small family.'"[10]

This division of labor, although widely recognized at the time, was often abandoned because of the shortage of domestic workers. During the mid-nineteenth century, housewives often complained that good help was hard to find. This feeling stemmed largely from the fact that native-born White women were disappearing from the ranks of domestic workers. During the period 1870 to 1900, the number of native-born White women engaged in domestic service decreased, while the number of immigrant White women increased. Domestic service became the purview of immigrant women, and Irish women, in particular, came to typify the average American servant.[11] The phrase "the servant problem" became synonymous with the facts that most domestic servants were transitory and were unfamiliar with the tasks required of them in middle-class households in an industrial society. But because so many domestic workers in the North were Irish, the phrase also had a subtext that signaled a range of differences between the new cadre of domestic workers and their employers relating to ethnicity, race, and religion.[12]

The nature of this servant problem varied by region. In the North, domestics were most often Irish, German, or Scandinavian immigrants, since the labor of racial or ethnic women was not widely available. In the Southwest, Mexican women dominated domestic service, whereas in the West, Chinese men, Japanese men, and later Japanese women dominated domestic service.[13] Although Black women were engaged in domestic service throughout the country, they dominated this occupation only in the South.

Employers complained that servants were indolent and inconsistent, coming and going as they pleased, but the need to retain a domestic servant was so great that such behavior was often tolerated. This flexibility is attributable to the high demand for labor. If domestics were uncomfortable in one place or thought the work was too much and the wages too low, they could simply find another situation. This behavior angered employers.

The servant problem was often construed as the Irish problem because the majority of domestic servants in New York were Irish women. The authors of the *New York Times* article did not mince words when describing the general dissatisfaction with Irish domestic servants:

> The influences that make Patrick and Barney a repeater, a riot-er ... percolate down to the kitchen and render Bridget and Kath-leen impertinent, shiftless, untidy, and gad-about, a steady invader of your larder, and sometimes of your wardrobe. These be harsh words. We confidently put it to almost any American housewife if they are not true words. Indolence and insolences are the faults of the Irish.... The class of which we are speaking, however, have such a monopoly of the servant market that they are fully able to get placed by assurance and by the fact that servants must be had rather than by their merit or by their popularity.[14]

The authors did not restrict their criticism to the Irish alone. "The Germans are the next most numerous of the female servants, and they labor under difficulties in American families, particularly at first. They do not understand our language, which can be taught to them, and they understand even less of our cooking, which it is questionable whether they ever fully learn.... The one drawback in their behavior is exces-sive sociability. It makes them excellent child nurses but bad kitchen maids.... They are faithful, strong and courteous, and a little inclined to 'slopping over.'"[15]

Black women, in stark contrast to both Irish and German domestic servants, were universally revered for their docility and willingness to work.

> Of the few [American citizens of African descent and Southern nativity] that have come up [North] the slightest tact makes most excellent servants. They do not have to learn to keep their "places" or anything especially new in affairs culinary. What they may lack in expedition and tidiness they well make up in the docility with which they hear suggestions.... In the not universal quality of kindness to children, they are simply excellent by the laws of their gentle, cheerful, grateful natures. They are the coming help, the servants of the future.... These colored people, for the present at least, have acquired few of the vices of the superior race of servants.

They develop and maintain strong local attachments, and they are so unconscious of the indignity of fully earning their wages that they are likely to do twice the work of other kinds of servants without regarding themselves overtaxed. Slavery was an excellent serving school beyond doubt, though a mighty bad moral school.[16]

The sentiment of the article is clear: away with the Irish, the German, and the Scandinavian and welcome the excellent Black servant of the South.

This wish was swiftly granted as a precipitous decline had already begun among White women in domestic service. Nearly 50 percent of all employed White women worked as domestic servants in 1870. By 1900 less than 25 percent were employed in that capacity, and by 1930 only 11 percent of all working White women were so employed. Growing disdain for domestic service on the part of native-born and immigrant White women and increased educational and occupational opportunities for those groups after 1900 led to their rapid departure.

In addition, this decline reflected the desire of White women to distance themselves from domestic service as it came to be widely characterized as the work of racial and ethnic women. Prior to 1900, there was a racial and regional delineation of the servant market such that White women dominated the North and Midwest and racial or ethnic minority women dominated elsewhere. However, in areas where racial or ethnic minority women were available to serve as domestics (Blacks in the South and Mexican women in the Southwest), White women were loathe to engage in domestic service.[17] In 1901, social scientist Virginian Orra Langhorne wrote: "When a Southerner speaks of servants, Negroes are always understood, [and] Irish Biddy, English Mary Ann, German Gretchen, and Scandinavian maids are as yet unknown factors.... Black Dinah holds the fort."[18]

After 1900, the racial and regional delineation of the servant market became increasingly blurred as racial or ethnic minority women, particularly Black women, became engaged in domestic service nation-wide. Unlike Black women's employment in farm labor, which was concentrated in the South, domestic service dominated Black women's employment in every region, with the exception of the South, until 1930.

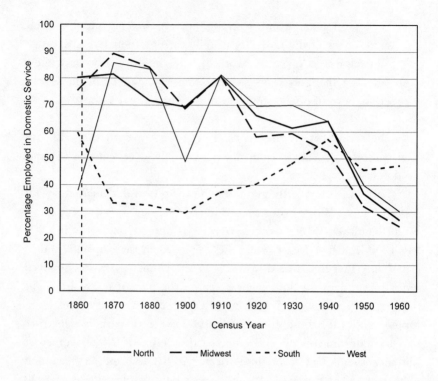

FIGURE 3.2

Proportion of Black Women Workers Employed as Domestic Servants by U.S. Regions, 1860–1960

SOURCE: Author's analysis of data from the Integrated Public Use Microdata Series, Version 5.0

While it seems a paradox that most Black women were domestic workers outside the South but not in the South, this trend is explained by southern Black women's access to other types of employment. Outside the South Black women were universally restricted to domestic service; their concentration in that occupation clearly reflects the absence of other opportunities. But in the South, farm labor dominated Black women's employment through 1920. After 1920, with the advent of mechanization in farming, the demand for manual farm labor greatly decreased and the majority of Black women found work as domestic servants. Once this occurred, domestic service became work for Black women regardless of geographic region.

Black women throughout the United States were restricted to domestic service—cooking in White kitchens, caring for White children, and cleaning White homes. In retelling the experiences of her relatives in Cleveland, Mary Helen Washington remembers, "In the 1920s my mother and five aunts migrated to Cleveland, Ohio from Indianapolis and, in spite of their many talents, they found every door except the kitchen door closed to them."[19]

By the end of World War I (1919), as White women were fleeing domestic work, Black women were on their way to dominating this occupation nationwide. While immigrant White women were starting to work in factories and native-born White women were moving into clerical work and sales, the only jobs available to Black women were as domestics or washerwomen. Even when levels of educational attainment were equal between Black and White women (both immigrant and native-born), Black women were generally excluded from sales and clerical positions except in small Black businesses.[20] Manufacturing, professional, trade, and clerical occupations became increasingly dominated by women as the twentieth century progressed, but Black women were excluded from these jobs on the basis of their race.[21]

Not only were Black women the only choice available for domestic service at the time, they were also more likely than immigrant White women to remain in service in spite of marriage. And because White domestic servants were unlikely to continue working after marriage, their turnover rate was high.[22]

Decreasing rates of immigration coupled with an increase in the overall ability of families to afford domestic labor lead to a great demand for domestic servants that outstripped the available supply. This inadequate supply was heightened between 1910 and 1920 when there was a sharp decline in the availability of household labor that is attributable to three factors: the low propensity of the women in the "new" immigrant groups (Russians, Poles, and Italians) to work, a decrease in the propensity of second-generation Irish women to work as household laborers (roughly 60 percent for the first generation compared to less than 20 percent for the second generation), and greater occupational mobility for immigrant women overall due to increased opportunities for education and the availability of sales and office jobs and teaching positions.[23]

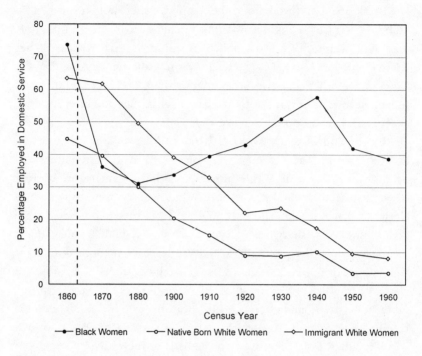

FIGURE 3.3

Proportion of Black, Native-Born, and Immigrant White Women Workers Employed in Domestic Service, 1860–1960

Source: Author's analysis of data from the Integrated Public Use Microdata Series, Version 5.0

Within the forty-year span from 1880 to 1920, Black women filled domestic service jobs as White women left the occupation. The proportion of domestic servants among native-born White women fell more than two-thirds in the period from 1890 to 1920, while the proportion of White immigrant women fell by nearly half. By 1920 only 9 percent of native-born White women and 22 percent of immigrant women workers were employed in household labor compared to more than 40 percent of Black women workers. Over the next forty years the proportion of both native and immigrant White women in domestic service continued to decline. In contrast, the percentage of Black women workers employed in domestic service increased steadily into 1940.

For White immigrant women, domestic service was a "bridging occupation" whereby they "acquired new skills, resources and values enabling them to experience social mobility."[24] This was possible because of their race: whiteness was the vehicle for upward mobility for White immigrant women rather than domestic service itself. But for Black women, domestic work was a permanent, lifelong occupation. Black women's entry into and domination of domestic service did not lead to greater occupational opportunity over the course of the next forty years.

The departure of White immigrant women from domestic service and the increasing entry of Black women coincided with a change in the function domestic work served for employers. Increasingly throughout the first half of the twentieth century, the ability to hire domestic help was a marker of status. Sociologist Judith Rollins argues that this is the main reason the employers she interviewed preferred to hire Black women.[25] There was no doubt that a Black woman in a White household was a servant. But her presence played into a racial hierarchy: the nature of the work and her relationship to her employer reaffirmed the employer's racial superiority.

Among domestic service workers, White women reached an all-time low of 4 percent in 1950 and remained there in 1960, a decrease of over 80 percent since 1900. By 1960, the percentage of Black women employed as domestic servants had fallen to about 39 percent, yet this reflects nearly a 14 percent increase over their representation in 1900 when farm labor was the only viable occupational alternative.

From 1900 to 1960, the ratio of the percentage of Black women to White women employed as domestic servants summarizes the extent of the overrepresentation of Black women. In 1900, the proportion of Black women and White women working as domestic servants for each of their respective groups was roughly equivalent, although it was tipping toward Black women. By 1910, the proportion of Black women workers employed as domestic servants was two times that of White women, and the disparity continued to grow every decade thereafter. By 1940, the proportion of Black women employed as domestic servants was five times that of White women, and in 1950 the proportion of Black women employed as domestic servants was ten times that of White women, an all-time high.

It is clear that Black women were actively restricted to domestic service. No other explanation sufficiently explains the divergent occupational paths for Black and White women. During this time period the gender segregation of occupations that increased opportunities for White women theoretically should have increased the opportunities for Black women as well. However, Black women's race prohibited their advancement in gender-specific fields.

OCCUPATIONAL MOBILITY DENIED

The restriction of Black women to domestic service was not a product of happenstance. Rather, Black women were often compelled into domestic service. The expressed goal of advocates of the New South during the period between Reconstruction and World War I was to "restrict Black workers' social and economic opportunities."[26] Black women who fled poverty and agricultural work and migrated from rural areas to urban centers, such as Atlanta, were segregated into household labor. Atlanta, the beacon of the New South, earned the distinction of employing one of the highest proportions of domestic servants in the nation from 1865 to 1920.[27]

After emancipation, employers resented Black women's attempts to exert control over the use of their labor and to engage in resistance by quitting at will, as Irish domestic servants did in the North. Instead of reacting with resignation, as did northern employers, who recognized their inability to force domestic servants to work, southern employers used coercion. When their attempts at dealing with recalcitrant domestic workers on an individual basis failed, employers petitioned the city of Atlanta for assistance.

In 1866, the Atlanta City Council responded, passing a law effectively prohibiting Black women from exercising freedom of choice in employment. This law made it difficult, if not impossible, for workers to easily change jobs by requiring employers to obtain recommendations from previous employers before hiring domestics.[28] The enactment of the law provides evidence that Black women were unwilling to quietly submit to exploitation. Yet quitting as a form of resistance persisted, as did the efforts of employers to control Black women's labor. These efforts intensified with the Great Migration during World War I.

Southern city councils manipulated "work or fight" laws, which were originally crafted in May 1918 to draft unemployed men into the armed forces, to restrict the employment options of Black women during a time of increasing opportunities for women in the sewing trades, in commercial laundries, and (to a smaller extent) in manufacturing. City councils abandoned the original intent behind such laws and instead used them to force women to work in jobs that contributed to the war effort. Women who pursed other employment were arrested. The laws were clearly gendered, but they were also interpreted along racial lines. "Work or fight" laws were used to punish Black women who left domestic service, because this work was said to be critical to the war effort in that it freed White women "from the routine of housework in order that they may do the work which Negro women cannot do."[29] A group called the "friends of the Negro race" in Macon, Georgia, argued that Black women should not withdraw from paid work in household labor because "patriotic duty" required that Black women not "sit at home and hold their hands, refusing to do the labor for which they are specially trained and otherwise adapted."[30] As a result, during the war, Black housewives who chose not to do domestic service work and even self-employed Black women, for example hairdressers, were arrested.

Even without direct help from the state, local communities mounted resistance to Black women's entry into more desirable occupations that were defined as "White" jobs. For instance, historian Elizabeth O'Leary documents an attack launched by the Housewives' League of Richmond in 1919 against the employment of Black women as waitresses in restaurants and stores. The league called on the city's Retail Merchants' Association to "request a substitution of White girls for the colored maids now employed as waitresses and in other capacities in order that Negroes may be released for domestic service."[31]

These were essentially local actions during World War I. But during the Great Depression, the pervasiveness of the attitudes toward Black women workers that informed them became federal policy. Federal funds administered through the Works Progress Administration (WPA) to provide economic relief through the creation of jobs were widely used to maintain established racial and gender norms that determined what jobs were suitable for Black and White women throughout the

South. Although WPA officials did not offer domestic service jobs themselves, they served as a conduit through which Black women were forced into domestic work. Lula Gordon, a Black woman on relief seeking work in San Antonio, provides evidence of this in a letter she wrote to President Franklin D. Roosevelt:

> I was under the impression that the government or W.P.A would give the Physical [*sic*] fit relief clients work. I have been praying for that time to come. A lady, Elizabeth Ramsie, almost in my condition, told me she was going to try to get some work. I went with her. We went to the Court House here in San Antonio, we talked to a Mrs. Beckmon. Mrs. Beckmon told me to phone a Mrs. Coyle because she wanted some one to clean house and cook for ($5) five dollars a week. Mrs. Beckmon said if I did not take the job in the Private home I would be cut off from everything all together. I told her I was afraid to accept the job in the private home because I have registered for a government job and when it opens up I want to take it. She said that she was taking people off of relief and I have to take the job in the private home or none.[32]

The role of the WPA officer as the arbiter of Lula Gordon's fate is clear. Southern Whites objected to Blacks being offered any aid, whether direct relief or public work, for fear that they would no longer be desperate enough to accept undesirable work on farms or in White homes. WPA administrators routinely refused to employ Black women in WPA jobs and acted as recruiting agents for private employers seeking domestic servants and even farm labor. In the rural South, Black women were told, "You can find work in kitchens," or "You can find work if you look for it." One Mississippi official told a Black women seeking aid to "go hunt washings."[33] The WPA circumscribed the use of Black women's labor to occupations that would reinforce the status quo.[34] Historian Jacqueline Jones argues, "Whether they were plantation owners or government officials, [whites] saw black wives and mothers chiefly as domestic servants or manual laborers, outside the pale of the (white) sexual division of labor."[35]

As late as 1940, the majority of employed Black women—about 58 percent—were employed as domestic servants, whereas only 11 percent of White women remained in this role. Historian Julia Kirk Black-welder, who studied three southern cities (Atlanta, New Orleans, and San Antonio) from 1930 to 1940, concludes, "The occupational data alone confirms that racial prejudices worked to confine Black women to domestic labor in the three southern cities regardless of the size of the Black population."[36]

Further evidence of the extent of Black women's employment restriction is provided by sociologists St. Clair Drake and Horace Clayton in their study of Blacks on Chicago's South Side in the late 1930s. They found that education did not guarantee Black women access to more desirable jobs and that the Black women they interviewed were fully aware of this fact. Recognizing that it was not skill but restricted opportunity that limited them to domestic work, they bitterly resented "a society which condemn[ed] them to 'white folks' kitchens."[37] Doris Walker Woodson recalls that "even sometimes with an education, you still had to resort to going back to that kind of work, something menial."[38]

Systematic study of the relationship of education to occupational opportunity confirms the experiences recounted in the individual accounts above. After taking educational attainment, regional distribution, urban/rural mix, and age into account as possible explanations for Black women's overrepresentation in domestic service, economists James S. Cunningham and Nadja Zalokar concluded that active discrimination played a more central role than any of the other factor in restricting Black women's opportunities. In the statistical simulations they conducted, Cunningham and Zalokar concluded that in the period from 1940 to 1980, even if all Black women workers had the same education and skills as White women, their occupational placement would have remained relatively constant because of racial discrimination; in their model, over 50 percent of Black women would have been employed as domestic servants.[39]

Even during World War II, a time of full employment, Black women were restricted to domestic service. Historian Laurie B. Green recounts the experience of Altha Sims, a Black woman seeking work in wartime Memphis, Tennessee. She was told upon visiting the Memphis

U.S. Employment Service office that "there was not defense work for [a] Negro woman," even though President Roosevelt had issued an executive order barring racial discrimination in war production industries a year earlier.[40] Frustrated by her inability to find work, Sims wrote a letter to the mayor of Memphis protesting her exclusion from defense jobs and insisting, "I want a Job but I don't [want] no cook job." Reporting that she had been told there was "no job for you but a skilet an pan," she asked, "Where would the Negro woman apply for work?"[41] The mayor replied, "I know of no positions for unskilled colored women other than domestic work . . . and I imagine that is why [the welfare director] told you that he could not give you a place."[42]

Black women were excluded from desirable wartime jobs, both skilled and unskilled, across the nation, not just in the South. The goal, it seemed, was to incorporate them sufficiently to meet labor demands but to employ them in roles that would not hinder them from returning to their true calling, domestic service. This was nowhere more explicit than in the South, of course, where observers reported that during World War II, "white wives exerted pressure on their businessmen husbands not to hire black women and in the process "'spoil' good domestic servants."[43]

White women from the middle and working classes were the true targets of wartime recruitment propaganda such as government posters and short stories in popular women's magazines aimed at filling White men's jobs. When Black women were mentioned at all in reference to wartime labor shortages, they were encouraged to enter service sector jobs in the industrial context—laundry and cafeteria work—that had been abandoned by White women as soon as more desirable opportunities arose.[44]

The use of Black women's labor throughout the country demonstrates blatant patterns of discrimination that began with emancipation but extended well into the 1960s. The seemingly universally shared sentiment that Black women were fit for undesirable domestic work and the willingness of agents at all levels to actively restrict their opportunities to enter more desirable occupations made domestic service an occupational black hole for Black women. There were multiple roads in, including economic necessity and legalized coercion, but no way out.

A LIFETIME OF SERVITUDE:
WASHINGTON, D.C., AN ILLUSTRATION

The papers of Myra Colson Callis, a social science researcher in Washington, D.C., in the early twentieth century, provides a glimpse into the past. Her research focused on women, work, and industry. In 1930, she participated in a study called *The Employment of Negroes in the District of Columbia*, which aimed to better understand increasing unemployment among Blacks and determine ways in which it could be abated.

Callis conducted and analyzed interviews obtained from more than 400 homes in which almost 1,000 domestic servants were employed, nearly 84 percent of whom were Black women. The pattern exhibited in Washington, D.C., was repeated in countless regions throughout the country. Of the nearly 32,000 Black women workers in that city in 1930, fewer than 6,000 were employed outside service occupations.[45]

Along with Black women's lack of employment alternatives, an explicit preference for Black domestic workers drove their overrepresentation, but Callis found that this preference was mitigated by the specific role they were expected to perform. White employers preferred Black women as laundresses, cooks, or maids for general housework, while they preferred White women as child nurses, parlor maids, and governesses.

When asked explicitly about their preference, nearly 80 percent of employers said that they preferred Black domestic workers. The rationale they offered for this preference was in keeping with hundreds of years of slavery and more than sixty years of Black women's restriction to domestic service. They told Callis that Black women were "better servants," "natural born servants," "obedient and respectful," "more easily managed or directed," "by reason of race, docile," "good-natured and willing to serve." Black women "keep their places," they said; they were "more devoted than White servants," "kinder to children and the aged," and "know how to respect White people." One respondent baldly described the racial hierarchy: "you want a servant to be beneath you."[46]

The sentiments expressed by these household employers in 1930 are strikingly reminiscent of those expressed in the 1872 *New York*

Times article written nearly sixty years earlier, which proclaimed that Black domestic servants were the servants of the future because they "do not have to learn to keep their places," "have few of the vices of the superior race of servants," and were admired for "the docility with which they hear suggestions" and their "universal quality of kindness to children."[47]

Callis developed a prototype of a typical domestic servant based on her many interviews that is much like the image of the Black domestic servant the *New York Times* had portrayed so many years earlier. She describes "a figure between youth and middle age, of brown complexion, healthy and strong, leaning towards the prevalent mode for slenderness and with educational qualifications falling between the sixth and eighth grades."[48] But by 1930, an even finer distinction had been developed that specified which type of Black women was preferred for which domestic role.

Skin color and size were not deemed important for cooks and laundresses, but these characteristics were central in choosing a chambermaid or waitress, although the preference for light- or dark-skinned employees was not consistent. Employer "A," says Callis, prefers a dark-skinned maid because "light ones are too stuck up," whereas Employer "B" wants someone who is "not too dark to handle food."[49] Although these skin color preferences were entirely irrelevant to the performance of specific tasks, they illustrate the degree to which employers were engaged in creating a particular image of servants in order to link subordinate racial identity and performance of a service role. The most common method of securing a domestic servant in Washington, D.C., in 1930, besides recommendations, was through an employment agency. Employers submitted requests accompanied on occasion by detailed descriptions of the work expected. One such request was submitted on October 3, 1939, by Mr. C. Douglas Sager on behalf of his wife. He wrote, "I am interested in obtaining an excellent colored laundress to begin work Wednesday, October 11th at 3826 Cathedral Ave, NW. . . . I am enclosing an information sheet which describes the work in detail."[50] (See Figure 3.4.)

Since Mr. Sager specified that he sought to employ a laundress, it is reasonable to assume that her primary responsibility would be the laundry. However, his detailed work description outlines a great

MORNING

Make beds, straighten bedrooms and baths, dust, mop, wash socks, clean shoes, change water in flowers, throw out old and replace with new flowers.

AFTERNOON

Wash clothes	Polish Brass and Silver
or	or
Iron	Wash floors and woodwork
or	or
Clean Baths	Clean Venetian Blinds
or	or
Vacuum	Scrub Kitchen Floor with hand brush

EVENING

Wash dishes, turn down beds, close venetian blinds, close pull curtains on all floors.

ANSWER THE TELEPHONE AT ANY TIME

HOURS	9:00 TO 8:00
	(Thursday and Sunday 9:00 to noon)
MEALS	lunch and dinner
	(Except Thursday and Sunday dinners)
WORK	usually according to above schedule, however, it may include any work of any nature requested by Mrs. Sager.
PAY	$50.00 a month. Paid every half month. Includes carfare.

FIGURE 3.4

Detailed List of Expectations of a Domestic Servant in the District of Columbia, 1939

SOURCE: C. Douglas Sager to the District of Columbia Domestic Employment Center for Colored, October 3, 1939, Box 193–42, Folder 8, Myra Colson Callis Papers, Moorland Spingarn Research Center, Howard University, Washington, D.C.

deal more than general washing. The day-to-day expectations of this domestic servant were quite onerous; seven days a week, eleven hours a day (except for Thursday and Sunday), in a flurry of constant motion to complete assigned tasks when at any moment additional tasks could be added. This schedule is for a laundress in a middle-class home (Mr. Sager was in real estate); such homes tended to employ more than one domestic servant to efficiently run the house. The work schedule does not include the tasks that might fall under another servant's purview, such as cooking and/or care of children.

However, it was not just the wealthy and members of the middle class who hired domestic servants. In fact, the majority of households included in this study, 218, were considered lower class. In lower-class homes, where having one domestic servant was considered a luxury, a maid for general housework would have performed all of the tasks that Mr. Sager specified, but for less money.

This pattern was not specific to Washington, D.C. The hiring of domestic servants was fairly commonplace across class lines nationwide by 1930.[51] Affluent families, middle-class families, lower middle-class families, and in the South even some working-class White families hired domestic servants. This was made possible by the pitifully low wages domestics were commonly paid.

Salaries for full-time general housework ranged from about $23 to $85 a month, or about $5 to $20 a week, but it was not uncommon for domestic servants employed in lower-class households to earn even less than this.[52] Employers who could not afford full-time workers hired part-time domestic workers who earned 19 cents an hour on average, while those who were employed for the full day earned on average 24 cents an hour.[53] Mary Anderson, director of the Women's Bureau of the U.S. Department of Labor in 1938, commented on the irrationality of the wage system in domestic labor. "In general, the employer does not consider the question: 'How much of a competent worker's time can I afford, at a rate which is socially just?' but rather 'Where can I secure a full-time worker for the amount I think I can afford to pay?'"[54]

Such irrationality was fueled by the racist belief that Black households could survive on much less than a comparable White household could. In addition, it was common for domestics to receive part of their wages in kind, in the form of leftovers from meals or old clothes. The assumption was that Black women and their families could make do on what White families no longer wanted. Maternalist assumptions pervaded the relationship between employers and domestics; the domestic was most often treated and ultimately compensated as a child rather than as a grown woman. The manner in which Mrs. Ruth B. Greig, a potential employer seeking a domestic servant, describes the matter of salary in a letter to a District of Columbia employment center on August 23, 1940, illustrates this point. "Now as to salary, I will pay her $7 plus car fare if she does not cook and eat supper. I will pay her $8 plus car fare if she cooks and eats supper. I shall increase her only on merit. I promise to do well by her but I want her never to beg anything of me. I'll give her what I want her to have."[55]

DOMESTIC SERVICE FOR MANY BLACK WOMEN was a lifelong occupation that was physically demanding and equally, if not more, emotionally taxing. Black domestic workers were subjected to explicit and constant messages that reminded them of their inferiority and their alleged suitability for the domestic role. Whites made it clear to Black women that domestic service was their highest calling and that it was to be performed with humility and deference. They were to know their place and gladly occupy it. They were expected to hide their anxieties and frustrations about serving a White family while temporarily deserting their own families with a smile and a willingness to work. These are but a few of the messages, all of which were constant, clear, loud, and deafening.

As late as 1960, nearly 40 percent of Black women workers were employed as domestic servants, compared to 4 percent of White women. Domestic service was women's work, but more precisely, it was racial or ethnic women's work. The performance of domestic work by Black women in White households reinforced age-old stereotypes about their servile nature, which justified their racial subordination.

As domestic servants Black women were simultaneously indispensable and devalued. Labor shortages prompted hysteria among White housewives, who could not imagine performing the tasks they asked Black women to perform daily. Many went to great lengths to ensure that a sizable domestic labor force was maintained, going as far as to request that White women replace Black women in more desirable occupations so that Black women could return to domestic service.

The trivial amount domestics were paid and the maternalistic practice of paying in kind with old clothes and leftover food demonstrates the extent to which both the person and the work were devalued. Although the work of domestics facilitated the leisure of their employers, the workers themselves, it appears, were dispensable. They were perceived as worthless, easily replaced, and childlike. The prevailing attitude of employers seemed to be "I will pay what I can spare and give what I don't want."

The racial dissimilarity of Black domestics from their White employers meant that the employers did not identify with the suffering of their employees. No job was too demeaning or demanding. Respect was nonexistent, and age was irrelevant; in the eyes of her employer, a 50-year-old Black domestic worker was still a girl and would be treated as such. Both the employer and the domestic were engaged in role-play in which occupational roles overlaid racial roles with exacting precision. Black women's ultimate departure from domestic service in the mid-1960s was due to a fundamental challenge to the racial order. Until then, both Black and White women were struggling—domestic servants to escape the drudgery of household labor and housewives to retain control of the Black servant and bolster their racial position in the process.

CHAPTER 4

Existing on the Industrial Fringe

BLACK WOMEN IN THE FACTORY

ALTHOUGH THE MAJORITY OF BLACK WOMEN remained mired in domestic service and farm labor through the mid-twentieth century, a significant number were able to leave the farm and ultimately the household to enter the world of factory work. Their transition, however, was a slow one marked by periods of progress and setbacks. Black women were prized as farm laborers and domestic servants, and industrial employers were hesitant to disrupt the "natural order" of things by providing them with an alternative to jobs that amounted to lifelong servitude. By no means was factory work ideal—it presented its own share of hardships—but it offered Black women benefits that were entirely absent in the other occupations available to them, including a degree of independence from employers, relatively consistent pay, set hours, and days off.

The late nineteenth and early twentieth centuries brought about innovation and industrialization that radically changed employment opportunities for unskilled laborers. The changes in the structure of the labor market heightened the distinction between skilled and unskilled laborers. It became the dividing line within the factory that determined men's and women's work and the worth of that work. Unskilled and semiskilled workers, laborers, and operatives were seen as easily replaceable, extensions of their machines, workers who did the preliminary tasks necessary for the machines to do the real work. In contrast, skilled workers or craftsmen, who were primarily White men, performed tasks that machines alone could not do. They often received specialized training and frequently supervised unskilled workers.[1]

Opportunities to work as craftsmen or operatives were largely limited to White men and women. Keeping Blacks in their place despite their newfound freedom was the stated objective of southern employers after the Civil War, and they accomplished this goal by preventing Black workers from entering new and more desirable occupations. However, Whites were perfectly willing to hire Black men for jobs that involved cleaning and heavy lifting; this practice did not challenge racialized conceptions of appropriate labor for Blacks.

Figures 4.1, 4.2, and 4.3 illustrate the extent of Black women's exclusion from factory work nationwide from 1860 to 1960, particularly the stark division between skilled, semi-skilled, and unskilled labor and the associated gendered division of labor.[2] Although most factory

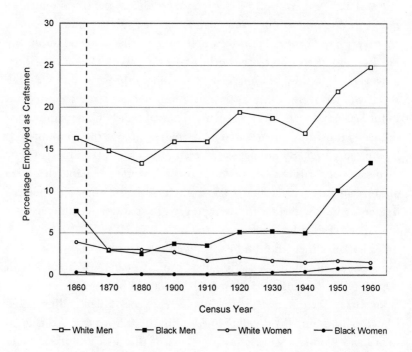

FIGURE 4.1

Proportion of White Male, Black Male, White Female, and Black Female Workers Employed as Craftsmen, 1860–1960

Source: Author's analysis of data from the Integrated Public Use Microdata Series, Version 5.0.

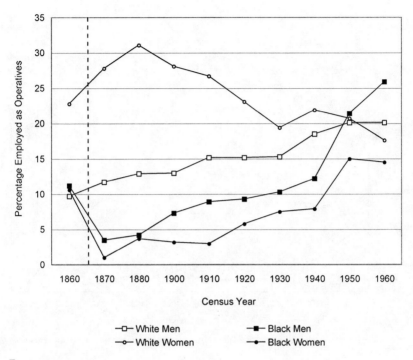

FIGURE 4.2

Proportion of White Male, Black Male, White Female, and Black Female
Workers Employed as Operatives, 1860–1960

SOURCE: Author's analysis of data from the Integrated Public Use Microdata Series,
Version 5.0.

operatives were White women, Black and White men also filled this
role. But Black women were rarely hired as skilled craftsmen. Less than
1 percent of Black women were employed as craftsmen in 1960, and
this is the high over this 100-year period. The picture for White women
is similarly grim; the nearly 4 percent of White women that worked
as craftsmen in 1860 is the high for the period. By 1960, less than 2
percent of White women were employed as craftsmen.

Yet the true significance of the occupational restriction of women
is not understood until you consider the vastly different economic
realities of craftsmen and operatives. Through 1940, virtually all women
employed as craftsmen escaped working poverty, whereas nearly half
of all White women operatives in 1860 and more than two-thirds of

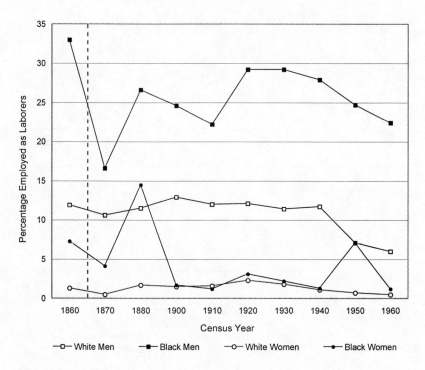

FIGURE 4.3
Proportion of White Male, Black Male, White Female, and Black Female Workers Employed as Laborers, 1860–1960

SOURCE: Author's analysis of data from the Integrated Public Use Microdata Series, Version 5.0.

free Black women were members of the working poor. However, not all operatives (that is, semi-skilled and skilled laborers) earned such low wages. Black and White men employed as operatives earned enough to escape poverty. In fact less than 1 percent of men employed as operatives from 1860 to 1960 were members of the working poor. Throughout the century the percentage of women operatives living in poverty declined fairly steadily, but it never reached the near-zero levels of men.[3]

The most salient criteria for employers when choosing labor and apportioning wages, it appears, were race and gender. Craftsmen were primarily White men, operatives through 1940 were primarily White women, and laborers were primarily Black men. However, these employment categories, which account for about 40 percent of all occupations, accounted for only a small percentage of all Black women workers. Less than 20 percent of all employed Black women in 1960 worked in these three broad occupational categories. Their underrepresentation in 1960, however, reflects a substantial improvement since 1940, when less than 10 percent of Black women workers occupied these jobs.

Deeply entrenched beliefs about racial and gender roles born during slavery were reproduced on the factory floor. Overseers—those who maintained the boundaries between groups and ensured that everyone remained on task—were White men. Black men worked on heavy machinery and performed arduous tasks, often carting raw materials through the factory. Clean spaces and finishing/packaging roles were reserved for White women, as concerns for their well-being and safety were paramount. Black women were most commonly employed to clean factories, but they were used for whatever jobs were unfilled.

As operatives, Black and White women had widely divergent work experiences. In 1860, twice as many White women as free Black women were employed as operatives. By 1870, the inequality was even more pronounced as the percentage of all Black women workers who were employed as operatives plummeted to 1 percent after emancipation. (This was because most former slaves were farm laborers in that census year.) In contrast, the percentage of all White women workers who were employed as operatives soared to nearly 28 percent. In 1880, the percentage of White women employed as operatives was eight times that of Black women. This stark inequality remained until 1920, when the percentage of White women employed as operatives started to decline as more desirable opportunities in clerical and sales work opened for White women. It was then that Black women operatives as a percentage of Black women workers began to rise steadily, as they filled the roles vacated by White women. Still, less than 10 percent of all Black women workers were employed as operatives until 1950.

The occupational picture of Black and White women operatives is full of contradictions. As White women left the occupation, Black women entered it. To White women, being employed as an operative was one choice among many options, while for Black women it was the only real alternative to the drudgery of domestic and farm work. Black women existed on the fringes of both the factory and the labor market, performing the most undesirable work, often under hazardous conditions with no possibility of advancement. Yet even the lowest-paying jobs in the factory represented significant progress from the farm and domestic labor sectors in which the majority of Black women toiled.

BLACK WOMEN IN SOUTHERN INDUSTRIES

Employers sought Black women workers as laborers in factories to do the work that other workers shunned or when no other groups were available. At the beginning of the industrial period, the decision to exclude Blacks from factory labor was primarily an economic one. During the cotton boom of the mid-nineteenth century, it was more profitable for slave-owners to use slaves to grow cotton than to sell their labor as factory hands. As a result, mill owners such as those near Athens, Georgia, "wanted to replace their slaves with Whites because White labor was cheaper."[4] After emancipation, owners of southern cotton mills refused to hire newly emancipated slaves primarily for racial reasons. Black women were thought to be incapable of working in the mills since Whites believed that they lacked the dexterity of White women and that they were "not temperamentally adapted to monotonous, mechanical work."[5] This, of course, was preposterous; slave-owners had used Black women in a variety of roles, both skilled and unskilled.

Excluding Black women workers from the cotton mills served to highlight the superiority of mill jobs and the White women who held them. Some employers did hire Black women in tobacco factories in large numbers, but many had no choice since processing raw tobacco was arduous work that took place in disagreeable environments for very little pay. Workers who had other options quickly abandoned such jobs. Only Black women were willing to tolerate these conditions, and that was because they had few other employment options.

White women working for pay drew the same scrutiny as Black women who chose not to work, particularly in industries such as tobacco that employed large numbers of Black women and men. In order to assuage the public's concern, employers had to guarantee that White women would not work at the same level as Black workers.[6] This requirement inspired a simple solution, the separation of Black and White women workers and the jobs they performed. Physical and occupational segregation allowed employers to address the concerns for White women's well-being while it simultaneously facilitated the exploitation and degradation of Black women. It also provided a justification for employers who were unable or, more often, unwilling to comply with the practice of separating the races in the workplace to exclude Black women from their labor force.

Southern textile mills maintained an almost exclusively White labor force until well into the 1960s. When mill owners hired Black women, it was only to fulfill their designated racial role. They essentially served as domestics in the industrial context—gathering waste or cleaning machinery—while White women performed the actual manufacturing jobs.[7]

Employers actively promoted racial antagonism and inequality. W. A. Erwin, a mill owner in West Durham, North Carolina, at the turn of the twentieth century, held a White supremacy parade in which White women in white dresses carried banners that said, "Protect us with your vote."[8] Employees were vociferous in declaring their opposition to integration. In 1896, an effort to integrate an Atlanta textile mill prompted a strike and the creation of a union headed by, and composed of, White women, who demanded that the Black workers in the mill be fired.[9] In 1919, a rumor that Black women would be hired in Macon, Georgia, prompted mob attacks on Black women that resulted in two deaths.[10]

Tobacco factories throughout the twentieth century, in contrast, were marvels of compartmentalization and provide a prime example of what the "inclusion" of Black women entailed. Black and White women occupied separate spaces in the factory and performed distinct work roles. Black women were hired to do the labor-intensive process of sorting, cleaning, and stemming tobacco leaves, whereas White women were hired as semi-skilled operatives who rolled cigarettes and inspected and packed tobacco leaves.

Although they were employed at the same factory, Black and White women experienced very different conditions. Black women were primarily engaged in the preparation of tobacco for manufacturing. When heads of tobacco first arrived at the factory they had to be cleaned. Workers shook out each bunch of tobacco to remove dust before removing sticks and other trash by hand. Blanche Scott quit her job in a tobacco factory after four years for health reasons. "When I left the factory, it became difficult for me to breathe. The dust and fumes of the burly tobacco made me cough. The burly tobacco from Georgia had chicken feathers and even manure in it. Sometimes I would put an orange in my mouth to keep from throwing up. I knew some women who died from TB."[11]

After being cleaned, the tobacco leaves were placed in steaming rooms to prepare them for sorting and stemming; these rooms subjected workers "to a high degree of humidity and to the heavy odor of tobacco."[12] Mary Dove, a former tobacco factory worker, recounts an episode when she fainted at work. "You know on the floor there was a salt dispenser, because it would get so hot. I did not feel so well when I came to work but I had to work. After about two hours standing on my feet, I got so dizzy—I fell out. My clothes was soaking wet from my head to my feet. When I woke up I was in the dispensary."[13] Pansy Cheatham, another worker, recalls that the factory "was so dusty that I had to go to the tub every night after work. There was only one window and it got so hot that some women just fainted. The heat and smell was quite potent."[14]

Stemming, or stripping, tobacco was the first step in the manufacture of cigars. Although this work was not skilled it required considerable dexterity since workers had to remove the midrib of the tobacco leaf, most often by hand, with as little damage to the leaf as possible.[15] When this work was done by machine, workers positioned the leaf under a knife that removed the midrib. Workers met the advent of mechanization with much despair. One woman exclaimed, "I don't think its right to put them machines to take away from us poor people."[16] More than concerns about being replaced, Black women were angered by the constant speeding up of machines as employers pressured workers to strip tobacco leaves at an ever-increasing pace. One worker recalls crying at the machine in dismay. "With them machines you have to thread the tobacco in. The machines run so fast that after you put in one leaf you got to be ready to thread the other. If you can't keep pace the foreman will fire you right on the spot. Sometimes I get so nervous but I keep on goin'."[17]

Annie Barbee, a former tobacco factory worker, angrily recalled the difference in the work environments of Black and White women. "You're over here doing all the nasty dirty work. And over there on the cigarette side White women over there wore White uniforms.... You're over here handling all the old sweaty tobacco. There is a large difference. It ain't right!"[18] Another factory worker, Rosetta Branch, said "They did not treat us black folks right. They worked us like dogs. Put us in separate buildings ... thinking maybe we were going to hurt those white women. Dirty work, dirty work we had to do. Them white women think they something working doing lighter jobs."[19]

In contrast to the anger and frustration expressed by Black women working in tobacco factories, White women workers were content with workplace and occupational segregation. One White employee voiced a sentiment shared by her co-workers: "Everything is running smooth all the time. We have good colored folks. They stay in their place; they don't bother anybody. They work around the plant stemming, cleaning, and that sort of thing, but we aren't with them."[20]

Historian Dolores Janiewski points out that segregating Black and White women in different jobs, on different pay scales, and in unequal work spaces was necessitated by the "rules of slavery," which were reproduced in the industrial setting and symbolically separated White and Black women into "superior and inferior beings."[21] White women could be hired only for jobs suitable for "respectable ladies," where "their racial and sexual 'honor' could be guaranteed."[22] No such constraint applied to the use of Black women's labor. Indeed, one employer boasted of his use of "brute treatment."[23]

Southerners were committed to maintaining the racial order, and exceptions to the practice of excluding Black women from factory employment altogether were permitted only in instances when factory labor reinforced racial roles. Black women were used in the factory to fill servile jobs that were the functional equivalent of domestic service in the industrial context, or they were hired to do jobs that were so dirty, hot, and otherwise disagreeable that no other group of workers would consider them. From the perspective of the Black women workers, however, anything was preferable to domestic work or returning to the farm.

BLACK WOMEN AND UNIONS
IN THE INDUSTRIAL NORTH

Southern employers did not have a monopoly on exclusionary labor practices in factories. Northerners also excluded Black women or severely limited their work opportunities. Although the majority of the Black population was concentrated in the southern states, from 1880 onward large settlements existed in the North as well.[24] Northern Black workers faced a challenge that their southern counterparts did not; they had to compete with White immigrants for jobs. In the South, there was almost no competition with other groups for the undesirable occupations. However, in the North, Blacks competed with White immigrants for unskilled work, the only industrial jobs to which Blacks were granted access.

The first wave of Irish immigrants came to the United States in the 1830s. Most lived in ghettoized neighborhoods in northern U.S. cities side by side with free blacks. They quickly began to resent their Black neighbors, who were their competitors in the labor market.[25] Irish workers became the enforcers of the racial order in the decades before the Civil War and often rioted to protest the hiring of Blacks. The racial status of the Irish themselves was not stable. Cartoons often portrayed Irish characters with ape-like features, and journalists and essayists routinely referred to "the Irish race," clearly defining the new immigrants as Other. "It was by no means clear that the Irish were white," historian David Roediger notes. But Whiteness was the basis for Irish Americans' entitlement "both to political rights and to jobs."[26] Thus, some Irish were very invested in separating themselves racially from Blacks.

Unlike English, Scandinavian, and German immigrants, who had access to more desirable occupational opportunities that were firmly closed to Blacks, Irish immigrants were largely confined to hard urban labor due to their lack of skills and capital and the anti-Catholicism of many northern employers. Roediger notes that "job competition has often been considered the key to Irish-American racism," but this view minimizes the influence of the desire of the Irish to become White and their perception that associating with Blacks would prevent them from achieving this goal. The Irish asserted their right to work because they were White, but they found it difficult to separate the fact that they did unskilled labor from the stigma associated with such work since it was widely defined as Black work. The solution they devised was to "drive all Blacks, and if possible their memories, from the places where the Irish labored." This contributed to the restricted occupational opportunities for Black men and women in northern states.[27]

Although northern employers were more interested in preventing the growth of trade unionism than in maintaining the racial order southern employers insisted upon, the outcome for Black women seeking work was the same—they were excluded from desirable opportunities and restricted to dirty and arduous jobs. But in the early decades of the twentieth century, a new industry emerged that provided a notable exception to the exclusion of Black labor in the North. The slaughtering and meatpacking industry had a great demand for cheap, unskilled labor. This, coupled with decreasing rates of immigration and the unwillingness of older immigrants to remain in undesirable jobs, led meatpackers to actively recruit Black workers from the South, going so far as to offer free transportation to those willing to leave.[28]

The arrival of these workers in northern labor markets coincided with the advent of deskilling in the meatpacking industry, where once specialized or skilled tasks, such as cattle butchering, were subdivided into an assortment of minute tasks that could be performed by unskilled workers. Skill was no longer a prerequisite for industrial employment. Instead, willingness to repeat rote tasks at ever-increasing speeds became paramount. These types of jobs were often poorly paid, were performed in unsanitary conditions, and offered no potential for advancement. Workers with options fled at the first opportunity. However, Black women's position at the bottom of the labor queue ensured that they were perpetually underemployed or unemployed and desperate for any opportunities available.

Although the Pullman strike did not have anything to do with the meatpackers directly, meatpacking employees joined a sympathetic strike two months later. Members of the newest immigrant groups—Poles, Austrians, Russians, Croatians, Serbians, and Hungarians—immediately began competing against one another to serve as strikebreakers. Four days after the strike was called, the company considered using blacks, but they decided against it. After a few more days, however, "[Negroes] were being brought into the yards."[29] The strikebreakers, both Blacks and new immigrants, enabled meatpackers to resume production without negotiating with the unions. Employers also found that the very presence of Black workers bred discord and strife among workers who were trying to organize.

The recognition by union organizers that the growing populace of unorganized Black and immigrant workers impeded their efforts led to the formation in 1897 of the Amalgamated Meat Cutters and Butcher Workmen of North America, which welcomed all workers—skilled and unskilled, women and men, immigrant and Black. For several years things were good, but in 1904 the union went on strike to set a uniform wage rate for unskilled workers. Union leaders said that "they struck to defend the under-dog, the rights of the men lowest and least protected in the industry."[30] It is an irony that the strike-breakers who enabled meatpackers to continue operations by replacing organized workers were the very ones for whom the strike was called, primarily nonunion common laborers: "Negroes, Greeks, Slavs, and Lithuanians."[31] Necessity, desperation, and ignorance of factors in trade negotiations led Blacks and new immigrants to work against their own class interests.

The use of Blacks as strikebreakers bred hatred and distrust toward them, and violent attacks by White workers were numerous. Blacks were beaten and assaulted on their way to work. Concern for minimizing labor interruptions rather than for Black workers' safety led employers to house Black workers in the factory. Policemen escorted them into the factory under the cover of night.[32] A crude representation of a Black worker was suspended from the crosstree of a telegraph pole at the entrance to the stockyards. "A Black false face and a placard pinned upon the breast of the figure bore the skull and cross-bones with the words "nigger scab" above and below in bold letters."[33] Although unions were also hostile to recently arrived White immigrants who served as strikebreakers, the racial distinctiveness of Black workers made them an easier target for the fury wrought on those who crossed the picket line. The monopoly of the Germans and Irish in meatpacking work was broken, and after 1895, "Lithuanians arrived, followed by a constant and increasing infiltration of Slovaks, Russian Poles, Greeks, Italians, and Russian Hebrews."[34]

After the 1904 strike, employers in the meatpacking industry deliberately used Black workers to foster racial divisions among workers. The following correspondence between officials of Swift and Company illustrates this fact:

Swift & Co., Denver File, Chicago, July 11, 1917. Swift & Co., #16Y, Denver, Colo. (Translation.) Answering: Want you to work closely with Hanson to prevent your house becoming organized, handling so as not to force a strike. Advise find cause other than being members labor unions for dropping two men mentioned or other active members and dispense with services as soon as practicable. Arranging have Mr. Jackson your house Thursday. Keep us fully posted. J. Burns.

Letter from Swift and Co., Denver File, Swift and Company, Stockyards Station, Denver, Colo., August 28, 1917; Mr. Louis F. Swift, President, Swift & Co., Stock Yards, Chicago. Dear Sir: Answering your letter of the 21st, regarding colored help at the Denver plant, we have recently started an Employment Bureau at the plant which will handle matters of this kind and we shall start at once to increase the percentage of colored help in the plant with the intention of getting it to 15 percent or higher as soon as we possibly can. Yours respectfully, Swift & Co., per J. B. Manager's Office.[35]

When interracial solidarity threatened employers' interest, they hired nonunion Blacks, a strategy designed to increase tension between Black and White workers, and dismissed pro-union workers in order to inhibit unionization.

For instance, the Chicago Federation of Labor formed the Stockyards Labor Council (SLC) in 1917 to coordinate the various unions in the Chicago-area meatpacking industry. Responding to the increasing presence of Black workers in the industry, the new council appointed several Black organizers in an effort to draw Blacks into unions. This strategy produced mixed results; Black workers protested that even when they joined unions, they were relegated to minority status, and some unions excluded them altogether. One strategy the SLC tried was forming an all-Black union, Local 651. Northern Black workers were willing to join this local, but southern Blacks were more reluctant, perhaps because of their deep knowledge of the perils of segregation. Despite these difficulties, the SLC was able to increase union membership in the Chicago meatpacking industry. By the end of the year, nearly 40 percent of that industry's workers had joined the union, which "issued demands for union recognition, wage increases, equal pay for males and females," and an end to employee discrimination on the basis of "creed, color, or nationality."[36]

Employers, recognizing the threat that growing interracial cooperation posed to their power, responded by firing union supporters and replacing them with nonunion Black workers.[37] The SLC responded two years later, in June 1919, with an intense campaign for "100% unionism." During the campaign, union organizers reached out to Black workers through Chicago's clergy and through mass meetings. Employers reacted to this new threat by again hiring more Black workers. In addition, they hired some Blacks to agitate against the SLC. Employers in the meatpacking industry repeatedly used Blacks to heighten racial tensions among workers and increase the racial divisions within the SLC.[38]

Employers hired nonunion Black workers for another reason; nonunion workers preserved the possibility that employers could continue production during strikes. Most resisted unionization so as not to jeopardize the few opportunities available to them. Northern Blacks, who were more familiar with the industrial system and the benefits of unionization, were more willing than southern Blacks to support union activity. Employers manipulated northern and southern Blacks with differing views on unionization and pitted them against each another, counting on their perpetual economic desperation as an incentive for them to resist unionization.

The interracial cooperation the Stockyards Labor Council exhibited was rare. It was much more common for unions to exclude Black workers. Despite the shared class interests of Black and White workers, many unions drew the color line sharply. Indeed, excluding Black men, sociologist Stanley Lieberson argues, "served to enhance the bargaining power of the unions," especially at the local level, and this practice persisted until the industrial movement in the 1930s spearheaded by the Congress of Industrial Organizations.[39]

Although the presence of new immigrant groups in the labor force invariably was associated with tension at first, after a period of assimilation workers were able to put aside their cultural differences and unite around employment issues. The presence of new immigrants from Southern, Central, and Eastern Europe in desirable industrial occupations meant that they "were eventually less shut out by the desirable craft unions than were Blacks."[40]

Black workers, on the other hand, never achieved a permanent presence in many industries, and in the industries that employed them they rarely advanced to craft positions. The vast majority remained unskilled laborers. And most Blacks who were hired as strikebreakers were not rewarded for their service. Inevitably, at the end of each strike many Blacks were let go and the bare minimum were retained. As social scientist Alma Herbst notes, employers "preferred White laborers and hired them to replace the Negroes whose service as strikebreakers was no longer required."[41] W.E.B. Du Bois argued that the great inequality observed between White immigrants and Blacks early in the twentieth century was due to strongly entrenched public opinion that quietly and at times publicly supported the economic restriction of Blacks. "[If there were not] ... an active prejudice or at least passive acquiescence in this effort to deprive Negroes of a decent livelihood, both trade unions and arbitrary bosses would be powerless to do the harm they now do; where, however, a large section of the public more or less openly applaud the stamina of a man who refuses to work with a 'Nigger,' the results are inevitable."[42]

THE WORST OF THE WORST: BLACK WOMEN'S WORK IN THE MEATPACKING INDUSTRY

No industry is more characteristic of Black women's relegation to undesirable factory work than slaughtering and meatpacking. The conditions of the work were extremely distasteful; workers handled raw meat, stood in pools of blood, and endured the cries of animals and loathsome smells. However, even in these conditions, Black women were relegated to the most unattractive and disagreeable tasks—hog killing and beef casing. In beef casing, where both Black and Polish women were found, Black women performed the more arduous tasks. They stood all day "at the sinks with running water, and inflate[d], inspect[ed], and grade[d] the casings," work that required training and experience, while the Polish women "cut knots from the casings with surgical scissors . . . work that is fairly simple."[43]

More often than not, Black and White women were segregated from each other. As in southern tobacco factories, this separation facilitated the placement of Black women in substandard facilities and improved the working conditions of White women. The differences were glaring. The work environment of Black women featured "long, slippery dark hallways and staircases leading from the most modern departments to dark, ill-ventilated rooms, not infrequently lacking a coat of White-wash or fresh paint."[44] Black women were barred from the more desirable positions, such as those in the pharmaceutical and gut-string packing departments, which were "clean, light, and comfortable."[45] In contrast, in the casing department, where wages were low and the conditions were poor, Black women predominated.

Race rather than skill determined the jobs to which workers were assigned, but gender handicapped Black women even further since slaughtering and meatpacking was a man's industry; only 15 percent of the workers were women, and of the women only 26 percent were Black. Further, the work that women were primarily engaged in—preparing the finished product for the market—was subject to much public scrutiny, which meant that employers preferred White women. One employer described his hesitation to employ Black women in this way: "The women cut and pack the beef. We must be scrupulous along sanitary lines and only White hands are fit to touch the meat. People would not buy our meat if they knew that colored women were employed. If we were a larger plant, we could watch the women more carefully, employing someone who did nothing but supervise them, but we cannot afford that. We could hire Negro women, but their hands would have to be washed almost every hour and we would have to manicure them."[46]

Other employers used the concern of the public about Black hands touching food products as an excuse for excluding Black women from certain jobs. One of the by-products of the meatpacking industry was butterine, a substitute for butter much like oleomargarine that was made with a combination of fat and milk. In one large establishment, Black women had been removed from the butterine room "in order that the question of Black hands touching the oleo would not be raised by plant visitors."[47] Another employer said that visitors' concerns about Black women performing "certain tasks in which fat grease and juice touch the hand" led to their exclusion from the butterine room, although no hands touched the product in the course of packing.[48] Yet another firm blamed the public for the exclusion of Black women from the "packing of bacon and chipped beef. It has never tried the public on this, but does not consider such an experiment worthwhile."[49] Another employer excluded Black women from the sliced bacon department. "Sliced bacon is one of the products in which the firm takes great pride; no expense is spared in its manufacture and distribution. Visitors, including all foreign guests and personal friends of the management, are always taken to the room in which the bacon is handled. The walls are painted white and the workers are clad in white. The employment secretary could find no other reason for excluding Negroes than that the picture might seem prettier to visitors if it were all white."[50]

It is ironic that while Black women were prized as cooks in White homes, public concern kept them from handling finished food products in the course of work outside the home. However, the blame for the exclusion of Black women from desirable jobs cannot be laid with the public alone. At one large firm where only 183 of about 10,000 workers were Black women (compared to 2,113 Black men), the superintendent flatly stated that he excluded Black women because "he did not like them. He had once been forced to take them because of a shortage in labor supply, and they were satisfactory workers, but his preference is for White women."[51] Such idiosyncrasies characterize the rationale for discriminating against Black women in the meatpacking industry.

Black women were not critically important to the overall functioning of the industry, but they were retained for two reasons: 1) their dependability during labor strikes; and 2) their willingness to do dirty work. The president of one meatpacking firm remarked that "we took the Negroes on as strikebreakers in 1921 and have kept them ever since in order to be prepared for any sort of outbreak."[52] The secretary of one company said, "We pay very little attention to the few [Black] women in our plant; they just do odd jobs."[53] She said that the six Black women who were employed in the company all engaged in glue stripping, "for no other women would do it. As we handle tallow, glue, soap and fertilizer, our factory has to be greasy, oily, dirty, and smelly."[54]

Despite the horrific conditions, blatant discrimination, and assured layoffs due to seasonality, Black women persisted in slaughtering and meatpacking. One employer interviewed remarked, "Negroes come back to our plant and stick by us. White people, if they have any ambition, soon find that there is easier work and better pay elsewhere and they soon leave us. Negroes are quite glad to get jobs in any factory."[55]

WORLD WAR I AND THE BLACK WOMAN WORKER

It was not until World War I that Black women were hired in significant numbers in northern factories. With the exception of the meatpacking industry, factory jobs were largely closed to Black women. However, the severe shortage of White men during the war years over-rode employers' tendencies to be selective about who they hired, and they were forced to use the workers that were available. The seemingly unending supply of new immigrants who served as a constant source of cheap and unskilled labor slowed as immigration to the United States declined rapidly during the war. In 1914, over 1.2 million immigrants entered the country, but by 1918, the number had declined to only about 110,000.[56] Out of necessity, employers began to explore alter-native sources of labor. They turned to Black men, White women, and Black women, but there was a hierarchy of who was hired to do what. White women were hired in the more lucrative wartime industries. Black men were recruited for jobs where the ability to perform heavy manual labor was a prerequisite.

Black women were universally recognized as laborers of last resort, a reserve labor pool that could be "drawn in when the economy expands or labor is needed for a short-term project, and pushed out when the economy contracts or the particular project ends."[57] Black women were an unmatched and untapped labor supply. Unlike Black men or White women, whose labor was restricted to either light or heavy manufacturing, respectively, Black women were adaptable to the needs of employers in either sector and were cheaper to employ. Further, Black women were willing to perform all tasks no matter how disagreeable, and it was socially acceptable or even expected for them to do so. Unlike White women, whose work was often limited to tasks deemed suitable for "respectable ladies," there was no constraint on the work Black women were expected to do, and employers were free to exploit them at will.[58]

Before the war, the number of Black women employed in factories was infinitesimal. Two studies commissioned in New York and Philadelphia to determine the extent and circumstances of Black women as industrial workers document the extent of their exclusion. The Philadelphia study, which was conducted from September 1919 to June 1920, opens with the following declaration: "This study has discovered no indication of any considerable number of Colored women being employed before the World War, outside of domestic service and those industries included in the term 'public housekeeping.' With the war came opportunities that brought a new day to this race."[59] The New York study, which was conducted in 1918, opens with a similar declaration: "Two years ago any discussion of Colored women in industry would have been met with the question, 'But are there any Colored women working in shops and factories?' And with good reason, for the Colored woman is a newcomer in the field of industry."[60] During the war, employers actively sought Black women workers for the first time. Newspaper headlines and articles reflected the expanding opportunities for Black women. One headline implored employers to "Use Negro woman labor to fill war workers' gaps"; another declared, "Negro's chance coming at last. Stoppage of immigration due to war strips South of colored labor."[61]

Black women could be found in almost every industry. No job was too hard, too dirty, or too demeaning. It was quite common, in fact, for investigators to discover Black women laboring in traditionally male jobs. In a waste factory, the Philadelphia study notes, Black women had replaced men in the task of "sewing up bales of the waste." This job required "continuous standing and working in unattractive surroundings, permeated with much dust." The employer remarked that this was work "that no White women would do."[62] Similarly, a newspaper reported that "Negro women are repairing railway tracks, making explosives, and serving as porters and inspectors in many industries here, taking the places of men who have gone to war or have entered other industries."[63] In New York the findings were the same. Black women were performing dirty, arduous labor typically done by men. "They were replacing boys at cleaning window shades, work which necessitates constant standing and reaching. They were taking men's places in the dyeing of furs, highly objectionable and injurious work involving standing, reaching, the use of a weighted brush, and ill smelling dye. In a mattress factory they were found replacing men at 'baling,' working in pairs, wrapping five mattresses together and sewing them up ready for shipment. These women had to bend constantly and lift clumsy one hundred and sixty pound bales."[64]

Even when employed in typical women's occupations, Black women did the jobs requiring the least skill, performing work under conditions that White women had rejected. Most often Black women were brought into direct competition with unionized White women workers to undercut or replace them. As employers in the meatpacking industry were doing, employers in other industries used Black women's labor as a threat to prevent the expansion of unionism. One employer, upon hearing that his Black pressers wanted to unionize, "threatened to discharge them if they did, and give their jobs to White girls"; another specifically hired Black women "because the White girls go out on strike so often."[65]

Despite the unpleasant nature of the majority of the occupations to which they gained entry and the low wages that barely allowed for subsistence, Black women left domestic service in droves for industrial jobs. White women who were formerly able to retain servants complained, saying that "their domestic workers had deserted them for their husbands' businesses."[66] Their complaints were not an exaggeration. Of the nearly 200 Black women workers interviewed in Philadelphia, 54 percent were former domestic servants. One newspaper article documented the trend: "Colored girls avoid housework. Y.W.C.A. is placing many in shops and factories, but few seek domestic service."[67]

However, Black women's departure from domestic service was tentative at best, since most had to alternate between domestic and factory work to make ends meet. One girl earned only $7 to $9 a week and paid almost $7 for room and board. She often ran out of money and would return to domestic service to save money before returning to factory work.[68] Yet the majority of women interviewed preferred factory work, citing "the freedom of the factory, the release from a personal boss, the definite and shorter hours, and the free nights, Sundays and holidays" as reasons why it was preferable.[69] Ultimately, however Black women's preference for factory labor did not create permanent change. After the war, most Black women workers were fired from industrial occupations and were forced back into domestic service.

Laborers of Last Resort: Black Women's Labor during World War II

As was the case during World War I, World War II prompted a severe labor shortage. However, the contraction in the availability of the labor pool employers preferred only led them to minimize, not do away with, restrictive employment practices. Historian Karen Tucker Anderson found that discrimination by employers persisted despite a shortage of the favored labor pool of White male workers. While it was the case that Whites were opposed to working with Blacks, employers did hire Black men. Anderson found that White men and White women had different motives for limiting the opportunities of Black workers and that these differences shaped the work opportunities for Black men and women. The prejudices of White men affected mostly the job opportunities of Black men because of the high degree of sex segregation in the labor force of the 1940s.

Employers who decided to incorporate women and Blacks into their workforce, she discovered, "established a complex hierarchy of hiring preferences based on the composition of the local labor force and the nature of the work to be done."[70] Employers preferred to hire Black men in industries that required heavy manual labor; they hired women only when there were not enough men to meet the demand. Employers in industries that required minimal manual labor preferred to hire White women.

"Whatever the hierarchy of preference," Anderson notes, "black women could always be found at the bottom.... Even some employers willing to hire white women and black men in large numbers balked at including black women in their work forces."[71] The intensity of discrimination is particularly noteworthy, since Black women comprised 60 percent of the Blacks who entered paid the labor force during the war years. Even during this time of full employment, the debilitating effects of dual subordinate statuses for Black women workers are evident.

The exclusion of Black women workers during World War II illustrates the impact of employer preferences on the occupational opportunities available to White women, Black men, and Black women. During this period employers had several options. They could recruit members of their favored labor pool from around the country or hire members of less-favored groups who were underemployed. Employers implemented a variety of strategies based on the intensity of their preferences.

Employers with relatively flexible preferences were amenable to hiring members of less-favored groups in a prescribed order, usually Black men or White women and then Black women. Employers with rigid preferences preferred to wait for a more desirable labor pool to arrive. For instance, historian Jacqueline Jones notes, "In late 1941 Kansas City defense plan personnel officers claimed they needed one thousand operatives but refused to hire the available Black women. Employers still preferred to await an influx of White southern migrants into the area, or to speed up their current workers, rather than take advantage of local Blacks who stood ready and waiting."[72]

The general reason employers gave for such blatant discrimination against Black women, Anderson records, was "the fear that white opposition to the change might cause work slowdowns."[73] Many White men were willing to hire Black men but unwilling to promote Black men to jobs with "higher skill and pay levels"; such actions prompted "most white male hate strikes."[74] Thus, Black men could frequently be found in industrial employment, albeit "confined to the periphery of the manufacturing process."[75] Regardless of their ability or tenure, Black men rarely advanced beyond entry-level positions. Hate strikes by White women workers, in contrast, could erupt if they were brought into "any contact at all with Black women."[76] White women's focus on a "desire to maintain social distance" required Black women's physical segregation, and when that was not possible, their total exclusion from the factory.[77]

As a result, physical segregation of Black women workers was a condition of their industrial employment. Gwilym A. Price, president and chairman of the Westinghouse Electric Corporation during the war, recounts that when Black women were hired at the beginning of World War II, "although no segregated facilities were provided, all were initially placed on the midnight shift."[78]

Employers who did not have the resources to physically segregate their labor forces routinely excluded Black women from jobs. A cost-benefit analysis often ensued by which employers "had to balance the cheapness of Black female labor with the high costs of physical segregation."[79] Thus, Jones notes, "larger factories segregated Black women in separate shops with inferior working, eating, and sanitary facilities. Smaller plants often refused to hire any Black women at all, if the provision of separate areas would have been inefficient or too expensive."[80]

When Westinghouse ultimately integrated Black women into their daytime shifts, "white women employees first refused to use the same washroom facilities as the Negro women and later, to work side by side with them."[81] The company appealed to the humanity of the White women, pointing to "their responsibilities as citizens and employees." More than this, however, "it was made very clear that, despite anyone's objections, management intended to see to it that Negro employees were allowed to exercise their basic rights as Westinghouse employees."[82] When employers chose to create an interracial workforce predicated on cooperation, their White employees had no choice but to comply.

Similarly, in New Haven, Connecticut, the Winchester Repeating Arms Company "simply told their female employees at the outset 'work together or else' and received 'fine cooperation' from them in return."[83] These examples of employer neutrality in a racially polarized sex-segregated labor market were the exceptions to the rule. Most industrial employers, Jones notes, acted on their preference for "white foreign-born workers (most from southern and eastern Europe) over the downtrodden blacks in their own country."[84] Blacks were "accorded a conditional welcome only after the supply of immigrant labor had diminished," or when labor shortages or political pressure necessitated that they be hired as temporary workers.[85]

As late as 1942, employers were adept at recognizing and conveying their reasons for excluding Black women. Common excuses given were "the plant did not yet have segregated bathrooms, there were not enough applicants for a separate shift of black workers, [and] white female employees would cause trouble."[86] Thus, even during the labor shortage of World War II, "the problem of racially segregating female employees" remained an important factor; as a result, generally, "employers hired either white women or black men first, depending upon industry, but black women always last."[87]

Although the hostility of co-workers was an important component of job discrimination, employers shared many of the racist and sexist beliefs and used the bias of White workers as an excuse to discriminate.[88] They often fanned the flames of antagonism by firing Blacks when there was the slightest workplace disturbance or by not hiring Blacks at all. For example, in 1943, an employer for an automobile manufacturer used a minor dispute in which a White woman took her Black co-worker's sandwich as the basis to fire four Black women who had just been hired and were not yet covered by union guidelines.[89]

Unionization was a key factor in determining Black women's occupational opportunities and the conditions of their work. Irene Branch, a former factory worker for the Firestone Tire Company, recalls how difficult it was before the union in 1944.

> When I first went in, they'd give the hardest jobs they could to the blacks. They'd give you the jobs a white person wouldn't want and you'd be making less money. It was really tough. You could be working side by side with a white person, and they'd get double the money that you got. You'd get less money, but you were doing the work, they weren't doing the work. But you had to take it, see! You couldn't do nothing else but take it or get going on, go somewhere else and get another job. . . . One place was as bad as the next, there was no use, if they didn't have a union. It was just rough."[90]

Once the union came in, however, things changed. Irene Branch described it vividly, exclaiming, "We didn't see freedom until we got that union in! We had to pay union dues, they'd take so much out of your salary, and that was OK. We had protection then, they didn't mistreat you."[91] Further, the union ensured that Black women could obtain supervisory and other desirable jobs for which they were qualified. Before the union, that would not have been possible. Irene Branch summarizes, "A black woman couldn't get a good job before the union. The white women could get good jobs, but a black woman couldn't get it. When we got the union, see, you could tell your steward what was going on, and how they treated you, and the union would make them be better to you. You had a right 'cause of the union."[92] However, the majority of the jobs to which Black women gained access during World War II were not unionized, and no one advocated on their behalf.

The postwar cutbacks of the General Cable Corporation in St. Louis illustrate the typical pattern of Black women workers' opportunities after more preferable groups become available. None of the Black women workers survived. In contrast, Black men "who benefited from the earlier integration into production work and the postwar bias in favor of male workers, constituted 16 percent of male employees in 1947 and could be found working in every job classification."[93] Similarly, Black men had worked at Westinghouse Electric Corporation since World War I, but Black women were not hired there until World War II.

BLACK WOMEN'S RELEGATION to the industrial fringe, often in jobs where they performed precursory steps in the manufacturing process, meant that their jobs were always vulnerable to replacement and erasure as technology and mechanization increased. Some of the work they did, such as tobacco stemming, was made obsolete.

Blatant discrimination against Black women was common across all industries until it was vociferously challenged in 1964. Prior to this, smaller victories were won because union intervention or civil suits, particularly after the desegregation victory of *Brown v. Board of Education* in 1954.[94] Evelyn Bates, a Black woman factory worker for the Firestone Tire Company, describes the change as follows: "The integration of jobs happened after the Supreme Court decision in '54. Before that, black womens couldn't be on the beads or nothing like that. Only thing a black woman could do in Firestone was sweep, work on the line doing heavy work like I was talking about, work up on the belt sweeping, where all that lampblack was, or clean the restrooms as a maid. They had a few black womens up in the cafeteria, on the black side. The white worked on the white side. That's all a black woman could do before they integrated the jobs."[95]

The stereotypes that had restricted Black women to farm labor and domestic service converged in industrial employment. Black women were perceived as capable of hard, back-breaking labor in jobs that were traditionally men's work. At the same time, they were seen as especially fit to fulfill in the factory the same role they had performed in White homes—sweeping and cleaning—performing the dirty but necessary work that kept the factory going. The degree of discrimination by race and gender was consistent across industries and across time. Black women received the lowest wages, labored in the worst working conditions, and were employed only when no other group of preferable workers was available.

CHAPTER 5

Your Blues Ain't Nothing
Like Mine

RACE AND GENDER AS KEYS TO
OCCUPATIONAL OPPORTUNITY

LABOR MARKET PRIVILEGE is inherently relational. It confers "certain privileges on the individuals and groups that oppress or are able to benefit from the resultant inequalities" and is fundamental to all forms of social oppression.[1] Racial oppression, for instance, is based on the relationship between White domination and Black subordination. Sociologists Melvin Oliver and Thomas Shapiro document this fact in their book *Black Wealth/White Wealth*, noting that an intimate connection exists between White wealth accumulation and Black poverty. Blacks have had "cumulative disadvantages," and many Whites have had "cumulative advantages."[2]

Similarly, gender oppression, which stems from the patriarchal structure of a society, results in a power imbalance that favors men. Sociologist R. W. Connell argues that gender oppression is pervasive and predates capitalist oppression but that both are intricately related, since "gender divisions are a fundamental and essential feature of the capitalist system; arguably as fundamental as class divisions" and "capitalism is run by, and mainly to the advantage of, men."[3]

However, society is not structured along the axes of race or gender oppression alone. Sociologist Eduardo Bonilla-Silva argues that "racialization occurred in social formations also structured by class and gender. . . . In these societies, the racial structuration of subjects is fragmented along class and gender lines."[4] Thus, the relational nature of race is complicated by the intersection of gender. Both are relationally constructed—Black/White, male/female—and they "gain meaning, in relation to one another."[5] Race and gender must be considered along a continuum that recognizes how individuals are gendered or raced according to the degree of privilege they have and the degree of their disadvantage; for example, whether they are members of a dominant or subordinate racial or gender group. This interlocking nature of oppression creates a complex hierarchy of privilege and disadvantage, in which, generally, White men are privileged, Black men and White women possess conditional privileges, and Black women experience near-absolute disadvantage. In all areas where there is a competition for desirable resources, the systematic exclusion or limitation of the racialized and/or gendered Other permits the advantaged group to preserve those resources for itself.

SEGREGATION AT WORK

In the world of work, all jobs are not equal. Some jobs are desired, some are despised, and all jobs tell us something about an individual's or group's personal and societal value, both real and imagined. In *American Work*, historian Jacqueline Jones argues, that "the work that people did, and the terms and conditions under which they did it, revealed both their place and their possibilities within American society."[6] Black women's restriction to undesirable occupations bears witness to this theme.

Prior to the passage of the Civil Rights Act in 1964, racist and sexist hiring practices produced a labor force strictly segregated by race and gender. Rarely were Black and White women or Black and White men found working in the same occupations. The existence of a racial hierarchy justified the unequal distribution of social goods (in this case occupational opportunities) among races by reference to their place in the hierarchical structure. The end result of this categorization was that opportunities for Blacks and Whites to improve their quality of life were dissimilar, and the high degree of racialization in American society is indicated by this dissimilarity in life chances.[7]

The segregation of Blacks and Whites and men and women across occupations was fundamental to the perpetuation of inequality. Groups are segregated by characteristics that symbolize dominant or subordinate status, thus providing the basis for unequal treatment. Sociologist Gunnar Myrdal notes that it is "the dominant group that

instigates segregation, sets its limits, and sometimes permits exceptions."[8] Occupational segregation can be seen as a result of the labor
queue, sociologist Stanley Lieberson argues, because employers' decision
to place group X high in the labor queue "results in group X being
concentrated in the best jobs and the non-Xs largely relegated to the
least desirable ones."[9]

In the early to mid-nineteenth century, occupational differences
among unskilled laborers were minimized, as there were few employment alternatives to agricultural labor and household service work.[10]
The growth of large-scale manufacturing, which signaled the transition
from an agricultural to an industrial-based economy, created an occupational hierarchy for unskilled laborers that formerly did not exist.
The advent of these desirable occupational opportunities, however, was
limited in its impact, as they were almost universally defined as White
men's jobs.

By the turn of the twentieth century, the practice of segregating
workers by gender was well established (see Table 5.1). Men dominated
the majority of occupations in 1900, although the extent of their
dominance varied. For instance, they composed roughly 97 percent of
all craftsmen and laborers but only about 63 percent of all professional
and technical workers. Their representation across the remaining broad
occupational categories, including managers, officials, proprietors, clerical and kindred workers, sales workers, operatives, and farm laborers,
fell within that range.

Women, however, were largely relegated to service occupations.
In the early nineteenth century, an ideology emerged that argued that
men should labor for pay in the public sphere while women should
focus on the private sphere of the household, where they should care
for their families and children. Historians refer to this as the ideology
of separate spheres. Popular magazines and other literature of the
period advanced the notion that a married middle-class White woman's
primary roles were those of wife and mother. Only unmarried women
were encouraged to work for wages, and their labor was restricted
to feminized or feminizing occupations, such as domestic service or
clerical work. Women were hired as paid workers only when the work
they performed conformed to the social mores of the day. Thus, in the
early to mid-nineteenth century, just as the North's industrial society

TABLE 5.1

Distribution of Men and Women Workers by Occupation,
1900 and 1920 (by percent)

Occupation	Men		Women	
	1900	1920	1900	1920
Professionals & technical workers	62.9	57.0	37.1	43.0
Managers, officials, & proprietors	92.9	93.1	7.1	6.8
Clerical & kindred workers	74.9	51.9	25.2	48.8
Sales workers	83.6	74.6	16.5	25.4
Craftsmen	97.0	97.5	3.1	2.5
Operatives	71.7	74.1	28.3	25.9
Service workers (household)	5.4	5.4	94.5	94.6
Service workers (nonhousehold)	57.8	63.4	42.2	36.6
Farm laborers	90.7	89.4	9.4	10.6
Laborers	96.4	95.7	3.6	4.3

SOURCE: Author's analysis of data from the Integrated Public Use Microdata Series, Version 5.0.

was emerging, the productive roles available to women decreased significantly in comparison to the wide array of productive roles they had filled in preindustrial society.

This pattern persisted throughout the nineteenth century. In fact, the only occupational category that women clearly dominated in 1900 (nearly 95 percent of all women workers were so employed) was private household service workers (see Table 5.1). Both men and women did service work outside the home, approximately 58 and 42 percent, respectively. Of all the occupational categories, nonhousehold service is the most misleading because it collapses a wide variety of occupational roles. Men, for instance, were more likely to serve as porters, elevator operators, and policemen, while women's roles were similar to those performed within the home—cleaners, beauticians, and waitresses.

The segregation of work roles into separate spheres facilitated the exploitation of women's labor as the majority of women were corralled into undesirable jobs and paid trifling wages. The notion of the "ideal woman" that the ideology of separate spheres produced prohibited women from competing with men for more desirable and lucrative jobs and necessitated that they withdraw from the labor market after marriage in order to devote themselves fully to their families. This exploitation of women's labor is a fundamental feature of the gendered social order, which has always privileged the labor of men over that of women.[11]

However, the occupational pattern observed for men and women in 1900 shifts radically when we consider the influence of race and men's dominance across occupations breaks down (see Table 5.2). The occupational picture for Black men in 1900 stands in direct contrast to that of White men, who dominated in all desirable occupational categories.

TABLE 5.2
Distribution of White Men, Black Men, White Women, and Black Women Workers within Occupational Categories, 1900 (by percent)
(Proportion of group employed in each occupation is in parentheses)

Occupation	White men	Black men	White women	Black women	% of all category
Professionals & technical workers	60.3 (3.7)	2.6 (1.4)	35.7 (11.7)	1.4 (1.5)	4.5
Managers, officials, & proprietors	91.8 (7.5)	1.1 (0.8)	6.9 (3.0)	0.2 (0.3)	6.0
Clerical & kindred workers	73.7 (2.0)	1.2 (0.5)	25.0 (6.0)	0.2 (0.1)	3.3
Sales workers	82.7 (4.9)	0.9 (0.5)	16.3 (5.2)	0.2 (0.2)	4.4
Craftsmen	94.4 (15.9)	2.6 (3.7)	3.1 (2.7)	0.0 (0.1)	12.3
Operatives	67.3 (13.0)	4.4 (7.3)	27.4 (28.1)	0.9 (3.2)	14.2
Service workers (household)	3.0 (0.2)	2.4 (1.4)	67.6 (24.7)	26.9 (33.8)	5.0
Service workers (nonhousehold)	46.0 (2.6)	11.8 (5.6)	27.6 (8.2)	14.6 (15.0)	4.1
Farm laborers	76.3 (36.2)	14.4 (54.4)	3.5 (9.9)	5.9 (40.1)	34.1
Laborers	78.7 (12.9)	17.7 (24.6)	1.7 (1.5)	1.9 (5.7)	12.0

SOURCE: Author's analysis of data from the Integrated Public Use Microdata Series, Version 5.0.

In fact, the proportion of White women employed exceeds that of Black men in all desirable occupational categories with the exception of craftsmen, which was considered heavy manufacturing and men's work. Operatives, on the other hand, worked in light manufacturing and could be both men and women. These labor patterns are in keeping with employer preferences. As historian Karen Tucker Anderson illustrates, Black men were preferred in industries that were manual labor intensive and women were utilized only if there were not enough men to meet the labor demand (see chapter 4). In contrast, White women were preferred in industries that required minimal manual labor. Black women were almost never sought except to perform industrial service.

The occupational picture for Black women is very different from that of White women. Both did domestic service work, but that is the extent of their occupational similarity. White women were well represented in all desirable occupational categories, whereas Black women were notably absent. Race was key to occupational attainment. White men and women worked in a wide range of occupational categories, from professionals to craftsmen, reflecting their access to desirable opportunities. In contrast, Black men and women were concentrated in a subset of occupations that closely mirrored their labor roles while enslaved. Nearly 90 percent of Black women worked in three occupational categories—farm labor, household service work, and nonhousehold service work—nearly all of which were undesirable. Race and gender combined to restrict Black women's opportunities. They did farm labor, as did Black men, and they did the domestic service work that was assigned to all women but was increasingly becoming their burden alone to bear.

The racial and gender differences observed in 1900 became more pronounced in 1920 as the labor market changed. Farm labor declined substantially, contributing less than a quarter of all occupations, compared to nearly 34 percent in 1900. Over those two decades, service workers in private households and laborers also declined as a percent of all workers, but by a smaller margin of roughly 1 to 1.5 percent each (see Tables 5.2 and 5.3). In all other occupations opportunities increased, some by a wide margin. The number of clerical and sales workers nearly doubled from 1900 to 1920. Overall, opportunities

TABLE 5.3

Distribution of White Men, Black Men, White Women, and Black Women Workers within Occupational Categories, 1920 (by percent)
(Proportion of group employed in each occupation is in parentheses)

Occupation	White men	Black men	White women	Black women	% of all category
Professionals & technical workers	55.7 (4.3)	1.4 (1.2)	41.9 (13.9)	1.1 (2.0)	5.7
Managers, officials, & proprietors	92.3 (8.6)	0.8 (0.9)	6.7 (2.6)	0.2 (0.4)	6.8
Clerical & kindred workers	50.7 (5.7)	0.6 (0.7)	48.6 (23.5)	0.2 (0.5)	8.2
Sales workers	74.1 (5.1)	0.5 (0.4)	25.3 (7.5)	0.1 (0.2)	5.0
Craftsmen	95.3 (19.4)	2.2 (5.1)	2.4 (2.1)	0.0 (0.2)	14.9
Operatives	70.2 (15.2)	3.9 (9.3)	24.8 (23.1)	1.1 (5.8)	15.9
Service workers (household)	3.1 (0.2)	2.3 (1.2)	56.1 (11.5)	38.5 (44.0)	3.5
Service workers (nonhousehold)	52.6 (3.1)	10.9 (7.1)	30.9 (7.8)	5.7 (8.0)	4.3
Farm laborers	77.0 (26.6)	12.5 (45.0)	4.5 (5.7)	6.1 (35.9)	24.4
Laborers	78.6 (12.1)	17.1 (29.2)	3.5 (2.3)	0.83 (3.1)	11.3

SOURCE: Author's analysis of data from the Integrated Public Use Microdata Series, Version 5.0.

in desirable occupations expanded and White women benefited largely from this shift. In 1900, nearly 75 percent of all clerical workers were men. By 1920, men and women were nearly equally represented among clerical workers, roughly 51 and 49 percent, respectively. Otherwise the gender segregation observed in 1900 remained fairly stable with men dominating all occupations with the exception of clerical and service work in private households.

The implications of these changes are further highlighted when we observe the distribution of workers across occupations by race and gender. When we consider only the top three occupations in which each group was employed, a large difference in the distribution of workers between 1900 and 1920 is evident (see Table 5.4). But equally telling is what stayed the same. Farm labor was the most important occupational category for more than half of Black men and over a third of White men in 1900. This was still true in 1920, even though the percentage of both Black and White men employed as farm laborers declined after 1900. However, this apparent similarity obscures real differences. While a small minority of Blacks in farming worked on their own land, most Black men and women farm laborers were tenants and sharecroppers who were coerced to remain on the land through a system of debt peonage (see chapter 2). In contrast, the majority of White men in farming (60 percent in 1860; 75 percent in 1960) were counted in the census as farmers (owners, tenants, or managers), not as farm laborers.[12]

TABLE 5.4

Top Three Occupations by Proportion of White Male, Black Male, White Female, and Black Female Workers in Each Occupation, 1900 and 1920

1900							
White men		Black men		White women		Black women	
Farm laborers	36.2	Farm laborers	54.4	Operatives	28.1	Farm laborers	40.1
Craftsmen	15.9	Laborers	24.6	Service workers[1]	24.7	Service workers[1]	33.8
Operatives	13.0	Operatives	7.3	Professionals	11.7	Service workers[2]	15.0
Totals	65.1		86.3		64.5		88.9

1920							
White men		Black men		White women		Black women	
Farm laborers	26.6	Farm laborers	45.0	Clerical workers	23.5	Farm laborers	35.9
Craftsmen	19.4	Laborers	29.2	Operatives	23.1	Service workers[1]	44.0
Operatives	15.2	Operatives	9.3	Professionals	13.9	Service workers[2]	8.0
Totals	61.0		83.5		60.5		87.9

1. Private household.
2. Nonhousehold.

SOURCE: Author's analysis of data from the Integrated Public Use Microdata Series, Version 5.0.

The second largest occupational category for Black men in 1900 was that of laborer. Nearly 25 percent of Black men in the workforce were employed in this category. For White men, the second largest category was that of craftsman; almost 16 percent of White men were employed in the highly skilled occupations that constituted this category. This divergent pattern also persisted over the next twenty years; in 1920, the proportion of Black men and White men in these two categories increased. For both Black men and White men, operatives (workers who performed unskilled and semi-skilled jobs) constituted the third largest occupational category. Roughly 7 percent of all Black male workers and 13 percent of all employed White men were operatives in 1900; these respective proportions increased slightly for both groups in 1920.

Overall the pattern observed for Black men and White men in 1900 remained relatively stable. Black men were channeled into unskilled work whereas White men were found largely in skilled and semi-skilled jobs. White male workers were distributed across all occupations; nearly 45 percent worked in occupations other than the top three categories of farm laborer, craftsmen, and operatives. Black men, however, found few alternatives to the three top categories for their group of farm laborer, laborer, and operative; less than 20 percent of Black men were able to find employment in other job categories. And none of the three categories in which they were concentrated offered skilled work, good wages, and a chance for advancement.

While occupational patterns for both Black and White men stayed stable during the period 1900 to 1920, White women and Black women had dissimilar experiences. White women embraced new opportunities in these decades, but Black women were given few alternatives to farm labor and service work. The differing experiences of the two groups of women was evident at the start of the period, in 1900. The top category shows the contrast in opportunities; over 25 percent of White women had moved out of household occupations and were working as operatives (see Table 5.4). In contrast, nearly 40 percent of Black women were farm laborers. The second largest occupational category for both Black and White women was service work in private households, although for Black women the proportion in this category was higher. More than one-third of Black women worked in domestic service, while roughly one-quarter of White women were found in this occupation. The third largest occupational category again demonstrates the vastly different opportunities for Black and White women. Nearly 12 percent of White women were professionals, largely teachers. But 15 percent of Black women were working as cooks and cleaners in nonhousehold settings, although the category of nonhousehold service work also includes personal services such as hairdressing. These three occupational categories account for nearly 65 percent of all White women workers and 90 percent of all Black women workers in 1900.

By 1920, Black women and White women did not share any categories in the top three occupations for both groups. More than 23 percent of all White women workers were employed in the growing field of clerical work; while Black women were almost entirely shut out of this occupation (less than 1 percent were employed as clerical workers). The second largest occupational group for White women was operatives; 23 percent of White women worked in that category. Again, Black women were virtually excluded from this category (only 6 percent found jobs as operatives). The third largest occupational category for White women was professional work. Nearly 14 percent of White women workers were professionals, compared to only 2 percent of Black women. The world of women's work was firmly divided by race by 1920.

While White women trended out of service work, solidified their presence as professionals, and entered the field of clerical work over these twenty years, the top three occupations for Black women stayed the same in the first two decades of the twentieth century. A small group (5 percent) were able to move out of farm labor, an occupation that still accounted for over one-third of all Black women workers, but the biggest change for this group was the 11 percent increase in domestic service work. This became their largest occupational category; 44 percent of all Black women workers did service work in private households in 1920. The third largest occupational category stayed the same—service work outside of households, although it declined to 8 percent, almost half the level observed in 1900. In 1920, just over 60 percent of White women worked as clerical workers, operatives, and professionals. White women in these occupations had moved out of domestic work and begun to enter fields that were new to them.

In contrast, in that year, 88 percent of Black women worked in the categories of farm labor, domestic service, and nondomestic service. These were the same categories that had been the top three groups in 1900, and the combined proportion of women in those three categories hadn't budged. Black women workers were clearly being excluded from the new occupations that were opening to their White counterparts.

These patterns for Black and White men and Black and White women were firmly entrenched and remained largely unchanged through 1960. The distribution of these four groups of workers across occupations was not random. It reflected beliefs about appropriate labor roles for each racial and gender group. Most White men were farmers and skilled or semi-skilled laborers, and this group benefited from the widest array of occupational options. White women were increasingly entering light manufacturing jobs in factories and pursuing professional jobs while fleeing domestic service. Black men persisted in farm labor but were gaining increasing access to jobs in factories for unskilled and semi-skilled workers. The occupational picture for Black women reflects the least amount of progress of all groups. The three largest occupational categories where they are demonstrate that they were limited to dead-end opportunities and excluded from jobs that offered better pay and a chance for advancement.

The field of clerical work provides a striking illustration of this disparity (see Figure 5.1). In 1860, less than 1 percent of all workers were employed as clerical workers. By 1960, nearly 15 percent of all workers were employed in this field. Less than 1 percent of White women were clerical or kindred workers through 1880, but by 1900, that proportion had increased to nearly 6 percent. In that year, the proportion of White women employed as clerical workers exceeded the proportion of White men in that occupation for the first time. After that the proportion of White women who worked in this field increased rapidly; by 1920, it had nearly quadrupled to about 24 percent. Their growth within this category persisted and by 1960 more than 33 percent of White women were clerical workers. No other group we are examining shared this pattern; White men showed a relatively flat pattern after 1910, and in 1960 only about 6 percent of White men were clerical workers. The proportion of both Black men and Black women increased slightly after 1940, but by 1960, both groups were still largely excluded; only 5 percent of Black women and about 8 percent of Black men were clerical workers in 1960.

It is clear that clerical work became segregated by sex as early as 1910 and that the typical clerical worker was a White woman. Although both Black men and Black women were employed in this field, the proportion of both groups was miniscule through 1940; around 1 percent or less for both groups during these decades. In 1950, there was a slight increase; the proportion for Black men reached about 3 percent, and the proportion for Black women slightly exceeded 4 percent.

The opening of new occupations in clerical work at the turn of the century changed the employment landscape for White women almost immediately, but it had no discernible effect on the occupational picture for Black women until 1950. Why? Entry into the feminizing

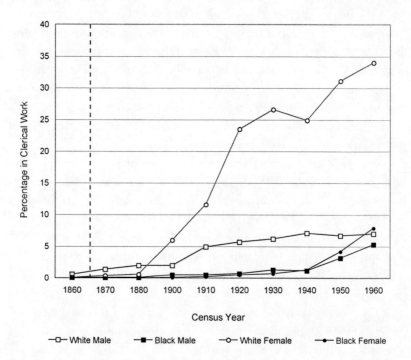

FIGURE 5.1

Proportion of White Male, Black Male, White Female, and Black Female Workers Employed as Clerical and Kindred Workers, 1860–1960

SOURCE: Author's analysis of data from the Integrated Public Use Microdata Series, Version 5.0.

occupations, such as clerical work, was based on objective and subjective criteria. All clerical and kindred workers had to complete high school, but they also had to be "presentable," and the consensus was that Black women definitely were not.[13] It is significant that Montgomery Ward, a mail-order business whose workers had no direct contact with their customers, was the largest employer of Black clerical workers (1,050 in 1920).[14]

The experience of Addie W. Hunter, a young Black woman who graduated from the Cambridge Latin and High School, is illustrative of the unfortunate and near-universal exclusion of Black women from clerical work. Despite completing the certification requirements that made her eligible for civil service and clerical positions in Boston, she worked in a factory. She waged a lawsuit in order to gain a position but was unsuccessful. In 1916, she remarked, "For the way things stand at present, it is useless to have the requirements. Color—the reason nobody will give, the reason nobody is required to give, will always be in the way."[15]

As late as 1946, social scientists Edward William Noland and Edward Wight Bakke found that nearly all employers in New Haven, Connecticut, and Charlotte, North Carolina, had strong preferences against hiring Black women. Noland and Bakke remarked, "No signs appeared over the employment offices of New Haven or Charlotte firms reading, 'Negroes need not apply.' But for all practical purposes that sign was out for clerical applicants to read."[16] Black women were barred from clerical work even when they had the requisite skills. The one place where Black women clerical workers had a good chance of being hired was in a Black business, and there were few of those. Clerical work was clearly typed by race and gender. White women moved rapidly and strongly into the new occupation. Black women were excluded.

Similarly, the growth of sales occupations had almost no bearing on Black women's occupational opportunities. Advertising experts told employers that "the most effective medium between public and product . . . was an attractive, well-spoken, and pliant young woman."[17] Beauty was for sale, and the underlying notion that salespersons must be White was understood. Increasingly aware of the public image of their businesses, employers who hired Black women did not allow them to serve on the sales floor. For example, a Chicago clothing store that employed both Black and White women in the 1920s used White women as salesclerks and Black women as maids.[18]

Julia Kirk Blackwelder's study of the three southern cities of Atlanta, New Orleans, and San Antonio from 1930 to 1940 illustrates how employers' racial and gender preferences determined occupational opportunities for workers. She shows how jobs for women in these three cities were typed by race and gender and that this greatly affected the workforce participation of women. To the extent that the typing of workers to occupations was flexible, racial or ethnic women did have some occupational choices. However, Blackwelder writes that as jobs that were strictly labeled by race and gender "rose or fell in strength, the number of jobs available to one ethnic group of female workers advanced or declined and labor force participation among that group manifested a consequent gain or loss."[19] For example, in Atlanta, as the number of white-collar jobs increased, the labor force participation of White women increased. When the number of domestic service jobs declined, the labor force participation of Black women declined. The same pattern was clear in New Orleans. In San Antonio, the number of domestic service jobs increased over the period of Blackwelder's study, and there the labor force participation of Black women did not decline.[20]

The strict racial typing of women's work largely precluded Black women's entry into desirable occupations. Less than 5 percent of employed Black women were professionals, managers, clerical workers, or sales workers in 1930 compared to more than 50 percent of White women (see Figures 5.2 and 5.3). While the percentage of Black women employed in these desirable occupations had grown to nearly 18 percent by 1960, that increase fell far short of the more than 60 percent of White women employed in those jobs.

Sadie Tanner Mossell Alexander, the first Black woman in the United States to be awarded a doctorate in economics, was unable to find work as an economist after graduating from the University of Pennsylvania in 1921. Excluded from White corporations because of her race and from Black colleges and research divisions of Black social service agencies because of her gender, Alexander accepted a position as an assistant actuary with a Black insurance firm in North Carolina. This

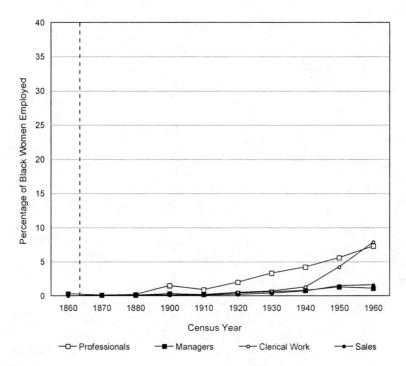

FIGURE 5.2

Proportion of Black Women Workers Employed as Professionals, Managers, Clerical Workers, and Sales Workers, 1860–1960

Source: Author's analysis of data from the Integrated Public Use Microdata Series, Version 5.0.

position, historian Francille Rusan Wilson notes, "was well beneath her educational achievements but [it was] her only permanent offer."[21] Reflecting on the fanfare surrounding her commencement, Alexander remarked, "All of the glory of that occasion faded, however, quickly, when I tried to get a position."[22]

Educated Black women such as Sadie T. M. Alexander often hailed from the middle class and worked not out of necessity but from a commitment to racial uplift. As sociologist Bart Landry illustrates for the period 1880 to 1950, unlike many White middle-class women, who typically left the paid labor force upon marriage, middle-class Black women persisted both in the public and private spheres after marriage due to their "threefold commitment to family, career, and social movements."[23] These Black women gained some entry into the feminized

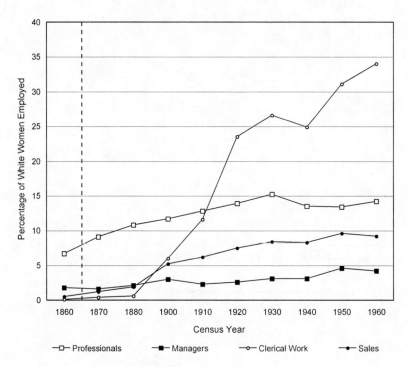

FIGURE 5.3

Proportion of White Women Workers Employed as Professionals, Managers, Clerical Workers, and Sales Workers, 1860–1960

SOURCE: Author's analysis of data from the Integrated Public Use Microdata Series, Version 5.0.

professions of teaching, nursing, and social work throughout this period, but race and gender were powerful constraints that were not ameliorated by class or education.

From 1860 to 1960 the structure of occupational opportunities in the United States changed in significant ways. Farm labor and domestic service declined while other occupational categories increased substantially. These include the professions, management, farm and business ownership, clerical work, and sales work. This growth transformed White women's work in particular, while the occupational options for Black women remained stagnant. Black men's access to these categories was similarly limited. However, Black men's exclusion from these categories was buffered by their increasing presence in traditionally male occupations, albeit in unskilled work roles as laborers or nonhousehold service workers, such as Pullman porters or elevator operators. While these jobs were not glamorous, they were typed as men's work and provided avenues for steady employment that were solidly closed to Black women. Amid the larger story of occupational expansion for White women and Black men, the routine exclusion of Black women is particularly notable and illustrates the centrality of both race *and* gender to occupational opportunity. The near-universal influence of racism and sexism on employers' hiring choices prohibited Black women's entry into new occupations and mired them in undesirable and devalued jobs.

PERSISTENT POVERTY

Occupational segregation allocates women, men, and racial or ethnic minorities to separate jobs and unequally distributes both the rewards of employment—income, benefits, and opportunities for advancement—and vulnerability to job loss. Additionally, it contributes to the persistence of a subordinate status for women and minorities in American society. It is commonly agreed that women are paid less than men and that Blacks are often paid less than Whites, even when men and women or Blacks and Whites occupy the same positions. But Black women suffer disproportionately in a system where their location on the either/or dichotomy of privilege associated with *both* race and gender relegates them to the lowest-paid occupations and positions.

In 1860, nearly all—94 percent—of free Black women worked in poverty-level jobs (see Figure 5.4).[24] No other group experienced such severe occupational limitation. In fact, the employment picture of free Black men for that year is quite rosy in comparison. The proportion of Black men in poverty-level jobs in 1860 was comparable to, and even lower than, the percentage of White men employed in poverty-level jobs. Although this is a snapshot in time and is mediated by the low sample size of free Black men relative to the large number of all White men in the labor force before emancipation, it is significant that even at this moment in time such an occupational picture was achieved.

After emancipation, the socioeconomic picture for Black women remained unchanged. When emancipated Blacks were included for the first time in census occupational data in 1870, 95 percent of Black women were found in poverty-level jobs, while the corresponding proportion of Black men increased to about 75 percent from their 1860 level of about 42 percent. Racial differences in who was assigned to poverty-level jobs heightened after emancipation. Prior to that, gender was the most salient marker of who got poverty-level jobs. Fewer men than women were employed at such jobs, regardless of the race of the man. However, in 1870, the proportion of Black men in poverty-level jobs surpassed that of White women. Thereafter race and gender interplayed, producing a new socioeconomic pattern in which men had lower rates of representation in poverty-level jobs than women of the same racial group.

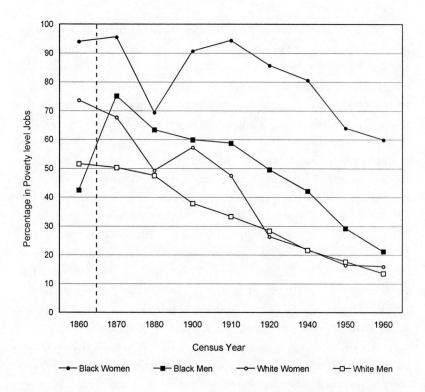

FIGURE 5.4

Proportion of White Male, Black Male, White Female, and Black Female Workers Employed in Poverty-Level Jobs, 1860–1960

SOURCE: Hayward Derrick Horton, Beverlyn Lundy Allen, Cedric Herring, and Melvin E. Thomas, "Lost in the Storm: The Sociology of the Black Working Class, 1850–1990," *American Sociological Review* 65, no. 1 (2000), adapted from Tables 2 and 3.

By 1880, the majority of White men had exited the working poor and White women soon followed, albeit not in a linear fashion. In the half-century after the Civil War, increasing numbers of Black men escaped poverty. By 1920, the only group of workers who was universally concentrated in poverty-level jobs was Black women.

From the 1870s through 1910, both Black men and Black women were limited to poverty-level jobs. However, by 1920, over 85 percent of Black women were still concentrated in such jobs, compared to about 50 percent of Black men. Although most Black men were still relegated to poverty-level jobs, some had gained access to more lucrative opportunities. This was never the case for Black women. Beginning in 1920 the proportion of Black women workers in poverty-level jobs was nearly double the proportion of Black male workers. By 1960, the proportion was three times greater than that of Black men. These statistics vividly illustrate the vast differences in Black women's access to occupational opportunity.

During the century from 1860 to 1960, all women had higher rates of representation in poverty-level jobs than men (see Figure 5.5). However, the story of Black women as compared to White women is one of relative hardship. At no point from 1860 to 1960 was the ratio of Black men to White men in poverty-level jobs more than two to one; the range was from 0.82 in 1880 to a high of 1.95 in 1940.[25] However, the ratio of Black women to White women in poverty-level jobs surged from a low of 1.28 in 1860 to a high point of 3.89 in 1950.[26] The inequality observed in the representation of Black and White women in poverty-level jobs reflects the increasing occupational opportunities for White women. These opportunities did not exist for Black women. Even as White men, White women, and Black men recovered from the ravages of the Depression during the wartime boom of the 1940s, the majority of Black women remained mired in poverty-level jobs, a pattern that persisted through 1960.

The dismal economic reality Black women faced for nearly a century was driven by a closed opportunity structure. Throughout a period of immense change and unparalleled growth in occupations, occupational segregation severely limited Black women's opportunities. In 1960, the majority of Black women labored in jobs similar to those they had held nearly a century earlier. This pattern sharply diverges

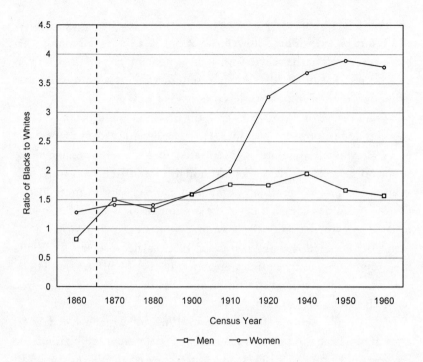

FIGURE 5.5

Ratio of Black to White Workers in Poverty-Level Jobs by Gender, 1860–1960

SOURCE: Horton et al., "Lost in the Storm," adapted from Tables 2 and 3.

from that of Black men and White women, whose occupational and economic distributions changed significantly over this time. While race and gender were central to defining labor roles at the turn of the century, the intersection of both race and gender led to a circumscribed opportunity structure for Black women that facilitated their exploitation for decades afterward.

JUSTIFYING RESTRICTED OPPORTUNITY: THE ROLE OF RACIAL IDEOLOGY

From the end of slavery to the dawn of the Civil Rights era, specifically 1860 through 1960, many aspects of labor changed in the United States. Blacks were transformed from coerced laborers to free laborers. Conceptions of women's work expanded from domestic service to include manufacturing, trade, and clerical occupations as well as the teaching and nursing professions. Agricultural labor decreased in its importance due to the rise of the industrial factory, which created an employment alternative for unskilled laborers. Increasing industrialization made some workers obsolete, such as laundresses, who were replaced by commercial laundries.

However, during this century of transformation, Black women's labor remained conspicuously unchanged. Table 5.5 illustrates the tenacity of discrimination, which marked service jobs—both in private homes and institutions—as Black women's work. In 1960, Black women were still largely excluded from professional work, clerical jobs, and jobs in factories. As Jacqueline Jones, one of the foremost historians of Black women's labor, has remarked, "The paid labor of Black women exhibited striking continuity across space—urban areas in the North and South—and time—from the nineteenth to the early twentieth century."[27]

For many decades after slavery ended, most Black women continued to do the same type of work they had performed before emancipation. A century after slavery had ended, nearly 40 percent of Black women nationwide continued to do domestic work. The majority of employed Black women did not exit farm labor until 1920. Even in 1930 more than a third were so employed.

At all times during the century from 1860 to 1960, these two arduous occupations were strongholds of Black women's employment. By 1920, the majority of White men and White women had been able to escape these occupations and the deleterious consequences associated with them. Black men were able to leave these occupational sectors later. Black women, however, were exclusively relegated to domestic service and farm labor, prohibited from entry into the growing occupational opportunities that were characteristic of the early twentieth century.

The jobs Black women did were some of the dirtiest, most arduous occupations at that time. It was not until 1950, when the demand for domestic service began to decline, that the number of Black women in these occupations fell below 50 percent. By 1960, nearly 100 years

TABLE 5,5

Percentage Change in Distribution of Black Women Workers across Occupational Categories, 1860–1960 (by percent)

Occupational category	1860[a]	1960	% Change
Professionals & technical workers	0.3	7.3	+7.0
Managers, officials, & proprietors	0.3	1.1	+0.8
Clerical & kindred workers	0.0	7.9	+7.9
Sales workers	0.0	1.6	+1.6
Craftsmen	0.3	0.9	+0.6
Operatives	10.6	14.5	+3.9
Service workers (private household)	67.4	38.5	-28.9
Service workers (nonhousehold)	6.8	23.1	+16.3
Farm laborers	7.0	4.0	-3.0
Laborers	7.3	1.2	-6.1

SOURCE: Author's analysis of data from the Integrated Public Use Microdata Series, Version 5.0.

[a]Only free Black women are represented in 1860.

after emancipation, over 40 percent of Black women, sociologist Carole Marks notes, were unable to escape "the old grips of slavery."[28]

Why does this matter? Farm labor and domestic service epitomized the occupational roles of those without choices over this period. Those who worked in these occupations could not make ends meet. Whether the worker was Black or White, a man or a woman, employment in farm labor or domestic service ensured abject poverty. The concentration of Black women in these occupations speaks volumes about the place and possibilities of Black women in the United States before the civil rights movement.

These occupations reinforced the image in the popular mind of Black women as servile and fit for dirty work. Jones describes the paradoxical nature of Black women's employment in these two occupations: it simultaneously confined them to farm/manual labor "so physically arduous it was usually considered men's work" and at the same time to domestic service, which was "vindictively termed women's work."[29]

Black women's racial identity as Blacks absolved Whites from affording them any of the protections society granted to White women. Further, their ability to labor as hard and as well as men confirmed the belief of many Whites that they were not women in the same way that White women were.

Sojourner Truth's "Ain't I a Woman?" speech delivered at the 1851 Women's Rights Convention in Akron, Ohio, illustrates the conundrum of Black women: they were biologically female but were excluded from society's definition of womanhood.

> That man over there says that women need to be helped into carriages, and lifted over ditches, and to have the best place everywhere. Nobody ever helps me into carriages, or over mud-puddles, or gives me any best place! And ain't I a woman? Look at me! Look at my arm! I have ploughed and planted, and gathered into barns, and no man could head me! And ain't I a woman? I could work as much and eat as much as a man—when I could get it—and bear the lash as well! And ain't I a woman? I have borne thirteen children, and seen most all sold off to slavery, and when I cried out with my mother's grief, none but Jesus heard me! And ain't I a woman?[30]

Indeed, the response to the question "Ain't I a Woman?" may seem obvious but was complicated by how a woman was defined in the mid-nineteenth-century United States. Psychologist Aida Hurtado points out that "the white women in the room [with Sojourner Truth] did not have to plow fields, side by side with Black men, and see their offspring sold into slavery, yet they were clearly women."[31] Although Sojourner Truth had borne children and could lay claim to one of the main functions of womanhood, that of motherhood, she was not perceived as a woman in the same way that White women were, and she was keenly aware of that fact.[32]

Many in the United States, from slave-owners to contributors to popular women's magazines to fiction writers, defined womanhood differentially in terms of race. For instance, a popular 1852 novel described the White heroine as seeming to be "little lower than the angels" with "an aureola of purity and piety" that "appeared to beam around her brow."[33] The views of a commentator for the popular magazine *The Independent* typify the attitude of many Whites toward Black women: "I sometimes hear of a virtuous Negro woman, but the idea is absolutely inconceivable to me.... I cannot imagine such a creature as a virtuous Negro woman."[34]

White womanhood was defined in terms of the "four cardinal virtues of true womanhood—piety, purity, submissiveness and domesticity," attributes thought to be absent in Black women.[35] Black womanhood was defined during slavery, when Black women were "required to be as masculine as men in the performance of work and were as harshly punished as men, but they were also raped."[36] In order to survive the brutality of slavery, sociologist Bart Landry argues, Black women had to develop characteristics in opposition to traditional conceptions of womanhood, such as "strength, rather than glory in fragility." They also had to be "active and assertive rather than passive and submissive."[37] These dual conceptions of womanhood based on race simultaneously permitted Black women's exploitation and White women's entitlement.

The exploitation of Black women in domestic service was similarly influenced by racialized conceptions of womanhood. Although domestic service was considered women's work, it contradicted notions of femininity. As Evelyn Nakano Glenn has observed, "Domesticity—defined as creating a warm, clean, and attractive home for husband and children—required hard physical labor and meant contending with dirt."[38] White women resolved their role conflict—achieving refinement in the home, which required hard, onerous labor—through the use of the labor of racial or ethnic women (and sometimes the labor of men in these groups).

Racial and ethnic women in domestic service could not be fully women in the way that White women were. Racial ideology justified the use of Black women's labor by asserting that they were "particularly suited for service" and were amenable to dirty, onerous labor.[39] Further, racial ideology justified the denial of Black women's shared womanhood with their employers. Thus the long hours (fourteen to sixteen a day) expected of the domestic servant, which prevented her from serving her own family as a wife or a mother, were not incompatible with the desire of the White employer for a clean and smooth-running household and well-cared-for children, since the family responsibilities of the domestic servant were inconsequential. White women's virtues were possible only because of Black women's labor. Racial ideology allowed Whites to reconcile their desire for clean and smooth-running households with the heavy demands they made of the Black women they hired to do domestic work. They simply didn't see Black women as women, wives, or mothers. To the White employers, Black women existed only as a source of cheap labor.

Asking the Wrong Question: Did Race Trump Gender?

The American occupational structure was and is deeply segregated by race, and the unequal distribution of Blacks across desirable jobs is rooted in the industrial transition. As work was being modernized, Black men and women were limited to archaic modes of labor, restricted to the farm and the household and actively excluded from the factory. Prevailing notions about what types of work were appropriate for women posed no challenge to employers; they had no qualms about the degrading labor options available to Black women. Any gender-based distinction about the types of work Black men and women should do had been erased during slavery.

The insistence of post-emancipation employers that these ideas should continue to be promoted is largely responsible for the extent to which Black women were denied the rights and privileges of womanhood. Their biological claim to womanhood was irrelevant; they were expected to work as hard as men unless they found themselves in women-only occupations such as domestic service. Black women were not protected and esteemed as White women were; instead, they were forced to perform demeaning work that was shunned by advantaged women.

Both Black men and Black women were generally limited to devalued jobs. Whether these jobs were devalued because Blacks held them or because they were undesirable jobs is debatable. Regardless, the consequences of employment in devalued jobs were severe. These jobs were often poorly paid, the work was performed in undesirable surroundings, and the work brought little opportunity for advancement. The relegation of Blacks to temporary or unstable jobs meant that they were perpetually under- or unemployed, which created a large reserve pool that employers could draw upon during labor shortages. Finding and keeping work was a perpetual challenge that was emblematic of the larger life struggle, "a struggle to survive in two contradictory worlds simultaneously," ethicist Katie Cannon argues, "one white, privileged, and oppressive, the other Black, exploited, and oppressed."[40]

Though Black women shared the burden of the consequences of racial oppression with Black men, they also shared the burden of the consequences of patriarchy with White women. The combination created a debilitating reality. Unlike Black men and White women, they could not draw upon a privileged status, such as manhood or Whiteness, to mitigate their disadvantage. Black women had a clear and unobstructed view of power hierarchies from the bottom. This unique position of marginality has meant that for Black women the struggle could not be defined solely in terms of either race or gender. The question "Did race trump gender?" fails to acknowledge the ways that both were intimately connected and shaped the work experiences of Black women. The gendered segregation of work relegated all women to less desirable jobs and the racial segregation of women's work defined all but the least desirable jobs as White women's work. Black women were confined to whatever work remained, the most devalued and undesirable jobs.

Some scholars argue that Black men face greater challenges in the contemporary labor market than Black women. Historically, however, Black women were clearly most disadvantaged. Of course, Black men faced obstacles, but the monumental challenges Black women faced points to the importance of distinguishing how their experience is unique. The combination of race and gender bias Black women encountered in the labor market marked them in ways that were separate and distinct from the experiences of their Black male counterparts.

The question "Who's doing better, Black men or Black women?" is also inadequate, since it fails to consider the ways that such a comparison oversimplifies the realities both groups face. For instance, if we consider historical periods, the difference in occupational opportunity is clear. Black men, both free and enslaved, worked in the skilled trades in the South during slavery. In addition to this, Black men occupied the same jobs as Black women—domestic service and farm labor—through the late nineteenth century.[41] But at the turn of the twentieth century, the rise of the industrial factory created new occupational opportunities for Black men, albeit limited ones. Black women were barred from these opportunities.

As the twentieth century progressed, Black men often referred to values of citizenship and manhood when they voiced their frustration about their exclusion in the labor market. During World War II, Black men were more likely than Black women to find defense work and to retain it after the war ended, although they were often relegated to unskilled jobs within that category. Clarence Smith wrote "What I really want is what a great portion of my race want: a chance to do something to help win this war and peace to come to every nation, to also win recognition in this our country, as citizens, human, and a important spoke in the wheel of progress."[42] While Black men and women shared the experience of being relegated to devalued jobs because of race, Black men could draw upon the universality of manhood as means of gaining and preserving access to work. For example, striking Black sanitation workers in Memphis in March 1968 carried posters that read, "I *AM* A MAN."[43] Dr. Martin Luther King, who was present at the strike, spoke to supporters and said, "We are tired of our men being emasculated so that our wives and daughters have to go out and work in the White lady's kitchen."[44]

The invocation of the principle of manhood in this strike, however, was more than an appeal to patriarchal privilege. It was a demand for respect that both Black men and women were routinely denied. Both resented being treated like children by White supervisors and city leaders. Hazel McGhee, a laundry worker, framed her own interpretation of the phrase "I am a man" that reflected her anger at the White foremen who treated Black women workers "like you was their child."[45] To McGhee, it was important that Black women support the gendered goals of Black men during the sanitation strike, which soon became a citywide strike of all Black workers. To her, the phrase also meant "that if she and other women could remain on strike for seven months, the sanitation workers too could be strong—that is, they could be men."[46] Rev. James Lawson explained the frustration of Black men in Memphis, noting that the city's mayor, Henry Loeb, "treats the workers as though they are not men, [and] that's a racist point of view. . . . For at the heart of racism is the idea that a man is not a man, that a person is not a person."[47] Both Black men and Black women shared the frustration that as grown men and women they were referred to as "boy" or "girl."

The employment challenges Black men and Black women faced were similarly shaped by racism, but they were differently influenced by gendered conceptions of appropriate work. Historian Laurie B. Green writes: "In the eyes of many black workers, racist employment practices perpetuated in modern urban contexts gendered, racialized constructions of labor based on the servitude and dependency that they associated with historical memories of slavery. While men reacted against being construed as laborers, helpers, and servants, women rejected images likening them to Mammy and Aunt Jemima, representations that had become central to advertising and film in the twentieth century and that called to mind the slavery era."[48]

Occupational segregation by gender is "one of the most enduring features of the U.S. labor market."[49] The exploitation of women's labor has been accomplished in different ways over time, but it has always functioned to privilege the labor of men over that of women, with the exception of reproductive labor, which is universally assigned to women, and more often than not to minority women.[50] The labor market privilege of men contributes to the "pay gap between the sexes and sex-based differences in job prestige, promotion opportunities, working conditions, and other work rewards."[51] Focusing on the experiences of Blacks in the labor market without disaggregating those experiences by gender disavows this reality.

This assertion is sometimes met with resistance because it suggests that Blacks are not uniformly affected by racial oppression and contradicts the view that Black men are the primary victims. However, we cannot ignore the reality of racism and sexism in the historical and contemporary labor market. As historian Manning Marable aptly notes: "From the dawn of the slave trade until today, U.S. capitalism was both racist and deeply sexist. The superexploitation of Black women became a permanent feature in American social and economic life, because sisters were assaulted simultaneously as workers, as Blacks, and as women. This triple oppression escaped Black males entirely."[52] The economic exploitation and subjugation of Black women was deliberate,

Frances Beale argues, since "the oppression of women acts as an escape valve for capitalism." She explains that "men may be cruelly exploited and subjected to all sorts of dehumanizing tactics on the part of the ruling class, but they have someone who is below them—at least they are not women."[53]

Beale described Black women as suffering from "double jeopardy"—dual discriminations of race and gender—but she did not address the question of socioeconomic class as another fundamental part of their oppression. Feminist Beverly Lindsay was the first to describe Black American women as "victims of triple jeopardy" because of their exploitation on the basis of race, gender, and economic class.[54] Sociologist Deborah King, in her critique of earlier conceptualizations of Black women's unique disadvantage, argues that class was not a "particular consequence of racism" but is instead an "autonomous source of persecution" that a majority of Black women experienced.[55]

It is necessary to challenge the cultural norm within the Black community that progress on racial issues is all that is necessary for true progress to occur. The class oppression that is the result of race- and gender-based oppression must also be challenged. "Sexism and racial bigotry are often so potent and so intertwined that they end up hidden within one another," resulting in a uniquely disadvantaged occupational and economic outlook for Black women when compared to Black men.[56]

The assertion that the reverse is true—that Black women have an easier time in the labor market than Black men—is false and a gross oversimplification of labor market dynamics. It reflects the sexist tradition that is alive and well within the Black community. Such assertions do not take into account the types of jobs Black women were able to get. The conclusion that White males "favored Black women over Black men" is illogical, Manning Marable argues, and is the result of the frustration of unemployed Black men who "perceived their wives' ability to gain employment as an assault on their own manhood."[57]

The types of jobs to which Black women have had an easier time gaining access have never been considered; the point that is always made is that they have had an easier time finding work. Race and gender segregation created appropriate types of work for Black women that were not considered appropriate for Black men; for instance, domestic service. An opportunity to work in an undesirable occupation is not the same thing as an advantage. Rather, it reifies a disadvantaged labor market position.

We must move beyond unsubstantiated musings about the influence of race and gender in the labor market. We can no longer treat the labor market experiences of Black men as being typical of the whole race. In doing so we hide the experience of Black women within that of Black men by assuming that gender does not matter. Nor can we examine the labor market experiences of women without disaggregating by race. In doing so we assume that race is not a determining factor. Nor can we ignore the economic class of workers in an occupation. To understand the labor market experience of Black women we must analyze Black women. Only when we take the multiple sources of Black women's oppression into account will an accurate picture of the influence of race, gender, and class in the American labor market emerge.

THE BLUES EVOKE SADNESS AND MELANCHOLY, dissatisfaction with one's state in life. Singing the blues has a long history in Black music, and there is no more fitting metaphor for the work experiences of Black women as it compares to that of Black men, White women, and White men. Hardship best describes the struggle of Black women to find and keep work from 1860 to 1960. Excluded from the social mores about womanhood that pertained to White women and restricted to jobs that were designated as Black, Black women were the victims of the race- and gender-based preferences of employers for other groups of workers.

While White women and Black men also experienced hardship in the labor market, it was different in kind and degree since each of those groups had a privileged status that buffered the impact of discrimination and granted them access—albeit limited access—to occupational opportunities. Black women were uniquely disadvantaged and were overrepresented in poorly paid occupations and nearly absent in more lucrative ones. Although both Black men and White men can sing the blues with regard to limited occupational opportunity, Black women can defiantly say "Your blues ain't nothing like mine."

CHAPTER 6

The Illusion of Progress

BLACK WOMEN'S WORK IN THE POST–CIVIL RIGHTS ERA

AFTER NEARLY A CENTURY of spotty occupational progress, the entire opportunity structure for Black women underwent a dramatic shift in the 1960s. In 1960, more than 60 percent of all employed Black women were in service work, and the vast majority, nearly 63 percent, worked in private households. One decade later, the proportion of Black women doing service work had declined to 42 percent, and of that group, 58 percent worked in nonhousehold settings. This change is significant, given the seemingly intractable association of Black women with domestic work prior to 1960.

However, the changes in the post-1960 period extend far beyond escaping the drudgery of domestic labor. Black women finally began making inroads into nonservice occupations from which they had historically been excluded. More than half of the Black women who were employed as domestic servants in 1960 (nearly 21 percent of all Black women workers) had exited by 1970. Although the percentage of Black women employed in nonhousehold service work, another occupation category Black women had been relegated to for decades, increased from 1960 to 1970, the change was slightly less than 2 percent. Hence, Black women did much more than simply change the surroundings in which they performed dirty work.

By 1970, clerical work, which hitherto had been reserved almost exclusively for White women, employed more than one-fifth of all Black women workers, more than two and a half times the proportion of Black women workers employed in that occupation category in 1960

TABLE 6.1

Change in the Distribution of Black Women Workers across Occupational Categories, 1960–1980 (by percent)

Occupation	1960 (%)	1970 (%)	1980 (%)	% Change
Professionals & technical workers	7.3	12.0	15.2	+7.9
Managers, officials, & proprietors	1.1	1.1	3.2	+2.1
Clerical & kindred workers	7.9	20.1	28.3	+20.4
Sales workers	1.6	2.6	3.2	+1.6
Craftsmen	0.9	1.5	2.5	+1.6
Operatives	14.5	17.2	15.5	+1.0
Service workers (household)	38.5	17.7	4.9	-33.6
Service workers (nonhousehold)	23.1	24.7	24.9	+1.8
Farm laborers	4.0	1.5	0.5	-3.5
Laborers	1.2	1.5	2.0	+0.8

SOURCE: Author's analysis of data from the Integrated Public Use Microdata Series, Version 5.0

and nearly five times the percentage employed in 1950. Additionally, Black women increased their representation in all occupational categories by a significant margin, with the exception of farm labor, which continued to decline, and management, where they held steady at 1960 levels. These shifts reflected a fundamental change in the allocation of occupational opportunities for Black women, and for the first time their occupational structure began to look like that of White women.

Table 6.2 presents the proportion of Black women employed in each occupational category compared to the proportion of White women, Black men, and White men in those same categories in 1960 and 1970. If the ratio is 1, then Black women are evenly represented in an occupational category relative to the other group. If the ratio is less than 1, Black women are underrepresented in an occupational category relative to the other group. If the ratio is more than 1, Black women are overrepresented in an occupational category relative to the other group.

In 1960, Black women were underrepresented in all desirable occupations where White women were found—professionals, managers, clerical workers, sales, craftsmen, and operatives. Although there was quite a bit of variation in the extent to which they were underrepresented, their exclusion from these jobs was consistent. There was a clear line demarcating what work was suitable for women based on race, evidenced by the fact that Black women were overrepresented in dirty jobs—domestic service, nonhousehold service, farm labor, and laborers. Domestic service provides the most striking example of Black women's relegation to undesirable work. In 1960, the ratio of Black women to White women employed as domestic servants was more than nine to one.

Despite the low ratio of Black women to White women in the most desirable occupations, a cursory glance at the comparable statistics vis-à-vis Black men (Table 6.3) and White men (Table 6.4) in 1960

TABLE 6.2

Change in the Ratio of Black Women to White Women Employed in Each Occupational Category, 1960–1970

Occupation	1960 (Ratio)	1970 (Ratio)	Change
Professionals and technical workers	0.5	0.7	+0.2
Managers, officials, & proprietors	0.3	0.3	0.0
Clerical & kindred workers	0.2	0.6	+0.4
Sales workers	0.2	0.3	+0.1
Craftsmen	0.6	0.7	+0.1
Operatives	0.8	1.1	+0.3
Service workers (household)	9.6	8.4	-1.2
Service workers (nonhousehold)	1.7	1.7	0.0
Farm laborers	2.7	1.9	-0.8
Laborers	2.4	1.1	-1.3

SOURCE: Author's analysis of data from the Integrated Public Use Microdata Series, Version 5.0

might lead one to believe that they were doing quite well. Instead, the high ratio of Black women to both Black and White men among professionals, clerical workers, and operatives signals the extent of occupational segregation by gender and points to the designation of these occupational categories as women's work. Although the ratio of Black women who were professionals to Black men who were professionals was more than two to one in 1960, the women were crowded into teaching. As sociologist E. Wilbur Bock concluded in his detailed study of Black women professionals in 1960, "Female professionals were highly concentrated in a few occupations, such as teaching, and Negro females appeared to be the most highly concentrated of all."[1]

Bock continued, "If Negro female teachers, social workers, and others in typically feminine occupations were to be removed from the total number of Negro female professionals; the total number of Negro professional men would appear in a more favorable light."[2] Segregation by gender is also clear in the data for the ratio of Black women

TABLE 6.3

Change in the Ratio of Black Women to Black Men Employed in Each Occupational Category, 1960–1970

Occupation	1960 (Ratio)	1970 (Ratio)	Change
Professionals and technical workers	2.3	2.1	-0.2
Managers, officials, & proprietors	0.7	0.5	-0.2
Clerical & kindred workers	1.5	2.7	+1.2
Sales workers	1.2	1.4	+0.2
Craftsmen	0.1	0.1	0.0
Operatives	0.6	0.6	0.0
Service workers (household)	48.1	44.3	-3.8
Service workers (nonhousehold)	1.6	1.7	+0.1
Farm laborers	0.4	0.3	-0.1
Laborers	0.1	0.1	0.0

SOURCE: Author's analysis of data from the Integrated Public Use Microdata Series, Version 5.0

TABLE 6.4

Change in the Ratio of Black Women to White Men Employed in Each Occupational Category, 1960–1970

Occupation	1960 (Ratio)	1970 (Ratio)	Change
Professionals, technical workers	0.7	0.8	+0.1
Managers, officials, & proprietors	0.1	0.1	0.0
Clerical & kindred workers	1.1	2.8	+1.7
Sales workers	0.2	0.4	+0.2
Craftsmen	0.0	0.1	+0.1
Operatives	0.7	0.9	+0.1
Service workers (household)	385.0	—[a]	—[a]
Service workers (nonhousehold)	4.4	3.5	-0.9
Farm laborers	0.5	0.3	-0.2
Laborers	0.2	0.3	+0.1

SOURCE: Author's analysis of data from Integrated Public Use Microdata Series, Version 5.0.

[a] Undefined value because there were no white men in household domestic service in this census year.

to White men across occupations. White men were underrepresented in the feminized professions, such as teaching, and overrepresented in the typically male professions, such as medicine, resulting in an overall pattern where Black women were underrepresented among professionals compared to White men.

Similarly, the overrepresentation of Black women in clerical work when compared to both Black and White men illustrates the feminization of this occupation. Employers routinely preferred women for clerical work, and their rationales were often directly tied to alleged innate characteristics. For instance, employers justified their hiring practices to social scientists Edward William Noland and Edward Wight Bakke by pointing to differences between men and women. Noland and Bakke characterized their attitudes in this way:

Men are more "active" than women and hence rebel at the monotony and sedentary character of clerical jobs. Women are "neater" and "more painstaking" than men and hence are better at detailed, repetitive, and small hand work. Women are satisfied with lower wages than men, and this type of work does not pay well. Men are "more ambitious than women" and hence would not stay on the job long, since some tasks are dead end, and those which are not lead to supervisory positions in which men are preferred. Women are "more pleasant and courteous" than men, and many jobs of this nature require these qualities. Women "accept supervision" better than men and this type of work must be constantly supervised.[3]

There were two exceptions to the nearly unanimous preference for women. First, if the clerical position required running errands and close contact with mostly male shop workers, employers preferred men. Second, in positions involving financial matters, employers felt that "men were likely to be more responsible" than women.[4] The overrepresentation of Black women in the field of clerical work when compared to Black men and White men reflects the fact that employers preferred not to hire Black men and White men. In contrast, in traditionally male occupations, such as craftsmen and laborers, so few Black women were employed relative to Black and White men that they were essentially nonexistent in those labor sectors.

All in all, whether compared to White women, Black men, or White men, Black women were concentrated in their own exclusive segment of the labor market—domestic service. In 1960, 38.5 percent of all Black women workers were domestic servants, compared to only 4 percent of all White women. This radical inequality is more pronounced when comparing Black women to Black and White men since less than 1 percent (0.8 and 0.1, respectively) were employed as domestic servants (see Appendix Table A.3). Although domestic service is traditionally conceived of as women's work, it was Black women's burden to bear almost exclusively.

By 1970, however, clear progress in what had been a rigid allocation of Black women to undesirable work is evident, as Table 6.2 shows. The greatest change occurred in clerical work, where the ratio of Black women to White women increased from 0.2 in 1960 to 0.7 in

1970. While Black women were still underrepresented among clerical workers, they made significant progress in shrinking the gap in what was at the time one of the most desirable occupations available to women. In addition, by 1960 more Black women had become operatives. This occupation had always included a small segment of Black women, but in that decade, it was the only occupational category in which they were nearing parity with White women. Ten years later, Black women had crossed the line of parity; for every White woman operative in the United States, there were 1.1 Black women. In the decade from 1960 to 1970, Black women also narrowed the gap in the field of professional work, while they decreased their participation in the fields of domestic service, farm labor, and labor (see Table 6.1). Yet despite the immensity of these changes, Black women were still greatly overrepresented in domestic service.

The story of change for Black women in 1970 is less encouraging when we look at the ratio of Black women to Black and White men across occupations. Nearly all of Black women's occupational gains were in women's occupations, and they lost ground when compared to Black men in managerial occupations. The great overrepresentation of Black women in domestic service relative to Black men remained in 1970, although it decreased slightly (see Table 6.3). No White men were employed in domestic service in 1970.

Unfortunately, the large decline in racial segregation did little to shake the longstanding segregation between men and women. Social scientist Edward Gross found that the occupational segregation by gender was fairly constant for the period 1900 to 1960.[5] Using data from a diverse sample of California establishments, sociologists William Bielby and James Baron found that gender segregation in 1970 was nearly total. Even when men and women were found in the same census occupation, they were "sorted into distinct organizations" or were "segregated by job titles within work settings." Hence, men and women almost never worked side by side in equivalent jobs.[6] Economist Mary C. King found that the dissimilarity indexes, which reflect the extent to which groups would need to change jobs to create evenness in representation within occupations, were "highest between Black men and White women and between White men and Black women." She notes that this data illustrates "the importance of both race and gender in the allocation of workers among jobs."[7]

Despite the persistence of occupational segregation by gender, the occupational picture for Black women continued to improve in 1980. Less than 5 percent of all employed Black women remained in domestic service, and not all of those who left that occupation were redistributed to nonhousehold service. More than 28 percent of Black women workers were clerical workers, nearly 25 percent were employed in nonhousehold service, 15 percent were professionals, and another 15 percent were operatives. Only about 3 percent of managers, sales workers, craftsmen, and laborers were Black women, while less than 1 percent of Black women were employed as farm laborers.

This marked improvement in the occupational distribution of Black women was reflected in their wages. In 1960, Black women earned roughly 65 cents for every dollar earned by White women, 67 cents for every dollar earned by Black men, and 42 cents for every dollar earned by White men.[8] By 1980, Black women had achieved parity with White women, earning 99 cents for every dollar White women earned, a reflection of their increasing access to White women's jobs.[9] Large gaps still existed with both Black and White men; most of the occupational opportunities and compensation available to men were closed to Black women. In 1980, Black women earned 79 cents for every dollar Black men earned and 61 cents for every dollar White men earned.[10]

While the rate of increase in Black women's wages surpasses that of all other groups for the period 1960 to 1980, that is because they earned the lowest wages of all groups in 1960. However, those low wages actually were a substantial improvement over the wages they had earned in 1940, when they earned 44 cents for every dollar White women earned, 62 cents for every dollar Black men earned, and 30 cents for every dollar White men earned.[11] Although Black women experienced the largest gains of any group in terms of income and occupation in the two decades from 1960 to 1980, perceptions of gains and progress must be tempered by an understanding of the severity of their occupational restriction prior to 1960. The fourfold increase in Black women's wages by 1980 must be understood in the context of their artificially low wages in 1940 and 1960 created by their severe underrepresentation in desirable and lucrative jobs. Although it would appear that Black women made significant progress from 1960 to 1980, in fact they simply began to catch up.

The optimism fueled by the steady economic gains of Black women in the 1960s and 1970s was dampened in the 1980s as reports of stagnating and declining wages for Black women began to surface. Economists Francine D. Blau and Andrea H. Beller found that older Black women who had formerly been concentrated in domestic service "had the largest increases in relative earnings of any gender-experience group over the period," due primarily to their occupational mobility.[12] But younger Blacks, both men and women, who had the highest wages in 1971, experienced declining wages relative to Whites in the 1980s. This trend, Blau and Beller suggest, began in the 1970s.[13]

Sociologist William Julius Wilson's controversial 1980 thesis that race was declining in significance as a predictor of economic status hinged on the success that younger Blacks had achieved in closing the wage gap in the 1970s. He argued that this trend would continue as the elimination of racial barriers provided a corrective to historical patterns of discrimination and that with better education the wage gap between Blacks and Whites would become a thing of the past.[14] However, the reverse happened and the wages of young Black workers declined in the 1980s.[15] Sociologists Becky Pettit and Stephanie Ewert document the erosion of Black women's wages since the 1980s: "Dramatic growth in the Black–White wage gap among young working women occurred in the 1980s. Among young working women, the wage gap hovered under 5% in 1979, widened considerably through the 1980s to reach a peak in 1990, and has fluctuated between 12% and 15% since the mid-1990s."[16]

Economist Augustin Kwasi Fosu argues that the initial gain in earnings that Black women achieved in the 1960s was a direct result of their occupational mobility. He notes that the trend toward higher earnings had slowed by the mid-1970s and that it reversed itself in the 1980s, especially when Black women's earnings are compared to those of White women. Fosu concludes that the "post-1964 occupational gains of Black women were episodic [limited to the earlier part of the post-1964 period], rather than long-term" and that Black women were stymied by the segmented nature of the labor market that granted them access to the White female sector but excluded them from jobs in the higher-paying White male sector.[17] King concurs: "By far the biggest reduction in occupational segregation by race among women occurs in the 1960s, when the measure falls by 25 percent.... Segregation continued to diminish rapidly through the 1970s. Very little change was apparent in the 1980s."[18]

Scholars agree that the occupational and economic gains achieved in the 1960s and 1970s eroded in the 1980s. But why did Black women advance into occupations when they did, and why wasn't this occupational progress sustained? Several factors—the passage of the 1964 Civil Rights Act, the post–World War II economic boom, and the growth of clerical work coupled with the decline of domestic service—undoubtedly contributed to the occupational advancement of Black women. To a certain extent, disentangling which factor was most responsible is irrelevant; the important thing is the progress that was achieved. However, understanding the multiple factors that precipitated Black women's progress is central to understanding why further progress was thwarted in the 1980s.

WHY PROGRESS?

The 1964 Civil Rights Act, specifically Title VII, which made employment discrimination on the basis of race or gender illegal in the United States, was revolutionary. It required a fundamental change in the ways employers went about their daily business. They could no longer use race as a determining factor in who they hired. Employers' preference for White women as clerical workers, for instance, was rooted in an assumption that White women were superior to Black women as workers. This stereotype about "Negroes' relative lack of desirable qualifications and relative possession of undesirable qualities" had persisted among employers, argued Noland and Bakke in 1977, because Black women were "practically excluded from jobs in which they would have the opportunity to demonstrate the inaccuracy of the stereotype."[19] Similarly, employers were convinced that Blacks were less capable than Whites on production jobs because they believed that "their intelligence is ... lower and their training less varied and adequate." Employers also believed that Blacks learned more slowly.[20]

Employers also perpetuated stereotypes about the personality of the Black worker. "The words unreliable, irresponsible, lazy, overbearing, unambitious appear frequently in Northern characterizations," Noland and Bakke reported.[21] Southern employers "found little necessity for applying such terms since they did not feel under obligation to justify any discrimination in preferences."[22]

Such discriminatory hiring practices became illegal on September 24, 1965, when President Lyndon B. Johnson issued Executive Order 11246, requiring businesses that contracted with the federal government to take affirmative action to ensure equal opportunity for employment. This set a precedent in federal employment practices. Section 202 states

> The contractor will not discriminate against any employee or applicant for employment because of race, color, religion, sex, or national origin. The contractor will take affirmative action to ensure that applicants are employed, and that employees are treated during employment, without regard to their race, color, religion, sex or national origin. Such action shall include, but not be limited to the following: employment, upgrading, demotion, or transfer; recruitment or recruitment advertising; layoff or termination; rates of pay or other forms of compensation; and selection for training, including apprenticeship.[23]

Although this was a monumental achievement, the evidence does not support the contention that the sweeping changes in Black women's labor allocation in the 1960s and early 1970s were solely the result of affirmative action.

In fact, as economist Jonathan S. Leonard documents, the U.S. Commission of Civil Rights, the U.S. General Accounting Office, and the House and Senate Committees on Labor and Public Welfare all agreed that during the 1970s, affirmative action was "ineffective" due to "weak enforcement and a reluctance to apply sanctions."[24] A 1975 report by the General Accounting Office found that enforcement of affirmative action policies by the contract compliance program was "almost nonexistent," which "could imply to contractors that the compliance agencies do not intend to enforce the program."[25] The most severe sanction of prohibiting noncompliant employers from participating in federal contracts was used "less than 30 times," and was not applied outside of construction contracts until 1974.[26]

Affirmative action policies were enforced much more actively in the mid- to late 1970s, but only for employers who contracted with the federal government. Those employers were pressured to comply with the policy and hire members of groups specifically listed in the act. But employers who did not do business with the federal government were not subject to penalties, and they often did not comply with the 1964 law with regard to the hiring of protected groups. Leonard found that from 1974 to 1980, the number of Black men and women "increased significantly faster in contractor establishments than in noncontractor establishments," and this pattern persisted even after taking establishment size, growth, region, industry, and occupational and corporate structure into account.[27] However, all employers, regardless of their relationship with the federal government, hired Blacks in unskilled positions. Black women, Leonard found, "increased their employment share in all occupations except technical, craft, and white-collar trainee." Affirmative action policies facilitated Black women's employment but not necessarily their advancement.[28]

Title VII of the Civil Rights Act, which allowed aggrieved individuals to seek legal sanctions and applied to all establishments, was significantly more effective at improving the occupational status of Blacks, especially Black women. Moreover, Leonard found that Title VII litigation "created pressure for occupational advancement as well as employment," as its impact was strongest "in the white-collar occupations, particularly in professional and management positions."[29]

The limited success of affirmative action notwithstanding, legal scholar Derrick Bell, Jr., questions the efficacy of the policy, writing that he has "serious doubt as to the long-term effectiveness and worth of equal employment laws."[30] He wrote in 1977 that "at present, the law channels charges of employment discrimination into a burdensome, conciliation-oriented administrative structure that functions, in the mean, on a case-by-case basis, depending on effectively-prosecuted litigation and a sympathetic judiciary for even the hard-won progress thus far achieved. Even the most wildly optimistic among us cannot reasonably hope that reliance on this complex and uncertain process will close the wide gap in income standards and unemployment rates between black and white and male and female employees."[31] Despite weak enforcement and reliance on the courts for setting legal precedents, economists Augustin Kwasi Fosu and Richard Freeman argue that government intervention in the labor market through affirmative action laws led in part to the improvements in the occupational placement and earnings of Blacks.[32]

This view is contested by other scholars who argue that the effectiveness of affirmative action was directly tied to employment growth. The representation of minorities and women significantly increased, Leonard found, "in establishments that were growing[,] and so had many job openings, irrespective of affirmative action."[33] Similarly, sociologists Kevin Stainback and Donald Tomaskovic-Devey argue that it is important to account for the growth of the economy since the 1960s when assessing the increasing numbers of women and minorities in managerial jobs. The number of jobs classified as managerial grew, beginning in 1966. The large number of jobs in this field enabled White men to maintain their advantage in managerial professions even as the numbers of minorities and women also increased.[34]

These findings point to the larger economic context of the 1960s as the catalyst for Black women's progress above and beyond the policy shifts. Did the widespread economic growth associated with the long postwar boom from 1945 to the early 1970s facilitate Black women's occupational progress? Some evidence exists to support the theory that it did, particularly the fact that Black women's occupational progress began in the 1940s. And their wages rose as a result; from 1940 to 1950, the average hourly wage for Black women doubled from $1.12 to $2.26.[35] If the post–World War II boom was responsible for Black women's increasing wages, however, we might expect that the wage increases would have continued in 1960. But they did not. Although the average hourly wage for Black women increased in 1960 to $2.87, the rate of increase had clearly slowed down considerably.[36] It is more likely that the earnings gains measured in the 1950 census were tied to occupational shifts as Black women left domestic service to enter wartime occupations. By 1950, the percentage of Black women workers in domestic service had declined to 40 percent (it had been 60 percent in 1940), but that statistic did not change much between 1950 and

1960. The fact that the next large decline did not take place until 1970 casts doubt on the idea that the post–World War II boom was the cause of Black women's occupational progress.

However, Black women who historically were underemployed and unemployed would have disproportionately benefited from job growth in the period of full employment associated with the boom, particularly given the larger sociopolitical context that encouraged equal employment opportunity in the 1960s. This prospect raises another question: Did job growth occur in the 1960s, and to the extent that it did occur was it in segments of the economy that Black women entered in large numbers?

By far the largest sector of the economy that Black women entered was clerical work. The proportion of Black women workers who worked in clerical and kindred occupations more than tripled from 1960 to 1980, from 8 percent to 28 percent. Economist Mary C. King's study of Black women's breakthrough into clerical work leaves little doubt about the connection between job growth and Black women's occupational mobility.[37] Between 1940 and 1960, the total number of clerical workers grew from about 7 million to nearly 10 million. Although this represents more than a 25 percent increase in the number of clerical jobs available, this increase is modest compared to the tremendous growth that occurred after 1960. In 1970, the number of clerical jobs surged to more than 14 million, double the 1940 number, and it continued this momentous upward climb, reaching over 18 million by 1980.

During this time period the labor force participation of White women increased but did not keep pace with the demand. King concludes that "fewer white women were potentially available to clerical employers during the 1960s than during any other decade since 1940. The watershed for black women's access to clerical positions came about at just the same time as the rate of increase in the labor supply of white women fell significantly behind the rate of increase in the clerical positions open to women."[38] As a result, employers did as they have always done in periods of labor shortage. They turned to workers lower in the labor queue.

The reserve labor force employers tapped to fill clerical vacancies was flooded with Black women rather than Black men because the conception of clerical work as women's work persisted. Hence, it seems that Black women benefited from the rapid expansion in the number of clerical jobs that merely coincided with the federal policy push for greater inclusion within the labor market, and it is not the case that affirmative action administrations oversaw a redistribution of a limited supply of clerical jobs. Further evidence for this thesis lies in the fact that the proportion of White women employed in clerical work also increased—from nearly 25 percent in 1940 to roughly 36 percent in 1980—alongside the dramatic gains observed for Black women.

While the passage of the 1964 Civil Rights Act, the post–World War II economic boom, and the growth of clerical work are just a few of the forces at work during this period, it is clear that they acted in tandem to facilitate the occupational advancement of Black women. Without this collective impact there would have undoubtedly been significant changes, but the effect would likely not have been as transformative in redistributing Black women across occupations.

The 1980s were marked by socioeconomic and sociopolitical changes that reversed some trends in Black women's occupational mobility. During that decade, the federal government stopped enforcing affirmative action laws, many industries experienced significant decline, the service sector became more prominent, the public sector declined, and the nation experienced an economic recession. All of these changes worked together to create new challenges that were not race or gender specific but that disproportionately affected Black women because of their vulnerability in the U.S. economy.

Progress Interrupted

While affirmative action was not solely responsible for Black women's occupational mobility, its role in challenging the normative climate of discrimination and encouraging remediation was undeniable. However, the success of affirmative action policies in improving Black workers' access to more types of jobs and to promotion within companies hinged on the political will to enforce them. The passage of the Civil Rights Act of 1964 alone was not enough to sustain change. After examining the impact of changes in the political will to enforce affirmative action on trends in workplace racial desegregation, sociologists Kevin Stainback, Corre L. Robinson, and Donald Tomaskovic-Devey conclude that "racial desegregation is an ongoing politically mediated process, not a natural or inevitable outcome of early civil rights movement victories."[39] The trend toward racial desegregation that began in 1966 did not continue after 1980, a clear sign that the political will had died.[40]

The election of President Ronald Reagan in 1980 marked a definite shift in the national climate. Suddenly, the laudability of the goals of affirmative action policies were open to question. While the Reagan administration was unable to dismantle affirmative action altogether, it fundamentally changed it from an active program to a symbolic one: there was virtually no enforcement after 1980. The impact on hiring practices among federal contractors was immediate. Leonard found that from 1980 to 1984, the rate of employment of Blacks and women actually grew more slowly at companies that contracted with the federal government than companies that did not do business with the government and thus had no obligation to hire employees from these two groups. At companies that contracted with the government, the rate of employment growth for Black men was 7 percent lower than expected. Leonard found that "the reversal for Black women was even more marked."[41] Milton Vickers, director of minority business development for Dade County, Florida, in 1985, remarked, "Most companies in the private sector are providing no more than lip service to affirmative action. There has been little monitoring for the past four or five years, and you can tell."[42]

Further, the Equal Employment Opportunity Commission, whose greatest impacts had been achieved through setting legal precedents, announced in 1985 "that it would move away from bringing suits aimed at helping entire classes of minorities and instead seek to remedy only individual discrimination."[43] This decision substantially decreased the commission's scope and influence. While the role of affirmative action in advancing opportunities for Black women before 1980 is debatable, the impact of the retreat from affirmative action after 1980 is irrefutable. Sociologists A. Silvia Cancio, David T. Evans, and David Maume Jr. document this fact, finding that the wage gap between young Black and white workers, both men and women, increased from 1976 to 1985. In 1985, "the White male advantage over Black men grew to 14.8 percent," while "white women earn[ed] 6 percent more than Black women."[44] The failure of the Equal Employment Opportunity Commission to enforce antidiscrimination laws, they conclude, "affected the hiring, pay, and promotion practices of organizations," and firms "discriminated against Black workers because the penalty for doing so was reduced or eliminated."[45]

However, the problems Black women workers faced beginning in the 1980s extended far beyond unchecked discrimination in the labor market. The structure of occupational opportunity changed. Cancio, Evans, and Maume confirm that "the growth of the service sector in cities failed to make up for the loss of manufacturing jobs, as service jobs were either low-paying jobs in personal service industries or high-skilled jobs in business and professional services."[46] The decline of manufacturing had a clear and decisive impact on Black women because they were concentrated in semi-skilled and unskilled occupations (operatives and laborers) that bore the brunt of displacement from 1979 to 1986. Many workers in these occupations lost their jobs when plants closed or shifts were eliminated. Very few of these women were reemployed in manufacturing jobs.[47]

Low-skilled Black women were particularly impacted by this shift. They were unable to find jobs that were comparable to those they had gained access to in the 1970s. The majority of low-skilled Black women were absorbed into the burgeoning service economy, which offered jobs characterized by low wages, no job security, and no health and retirement benefits.[48] Many of these were part-time jobs.

Although Black women were more likely to work full time than were White women, according to Petit and Ewert, "they are overrepresented in occupations that are more likely to be both part-time and poorly paid."[49] However, in an economy that increasingly emphasized educational qualifications, low-skilled Black women had few options in the job market. Further, competition for all jobs increased as Black men lost ground in industrial occupations and immigration increased the pool of low-wage labor from which employers could draw.[50] The rapid decline of manufacturing as an employment option effectively closed the door to the primary labor market for low-skilled Black women.

While educated Black women fared better than low-skilled Black women in the 1980s, in an economy in which corporate restructuring was on the rise, they were not immune to job displacement.

Professional Black women were subject to layoffs because of mergers and other economic downturns, but they were better able to land on their feet than their low-skilled counterparts.[51]

But overall, the job security of educated Black women was tenuous at best because they were disproportionately found in public sector jobs.[52] Economist Lynn C. Burbridge documents Black women's over-reliance on government work. From 1950 to 1970, the proportion of government workers among all workers grew by 44 percent, but the percentage of Black women government workers as a percentage of all workers grew by 140 percent.[53] From 1970 to 1990, the percentage of government workers relative to all workers declined by 6 percent, but the percent of Black women government workers as a percentage of all workers increased by 7 percent despite the overall decline.[54]

Black women sought work in the public sector to escape the pervasive discrimination within the private sector. Among women, for instance, King notes, "The private sector remained more segregated [by sex] in 1988 than the public sector had been in 1940."[55] Burbridge found that in the 1990s fully 85 percent of professional Black women worked in industries—health, social services, and education—that were dominated by government and/or nonprofit employment.[56] This over-representation in public sector employment meant that Black women were extremely vulnerable to policy shifts and budget cuts. Sociologists Yvonne D. Newsome and F. Nii-Amoo Dodoo found that from 1980 to 1990, the proportion of Black women in public sector jobs declined from nearly 32 to roughly 28 percent.[57]

The declines low-skilled Black women experienced in manu-facturing and skilled Black women experienced in the public sector had a great impact on the wages of these two groups. Wage inequality between Black women and White women had decreased during the mid-1970s, but by 1990, the trend had reversed sharply. Econo-mists John Bound and Laura Dresser estimate that by 1991, "African American women's wages lagged 14 percent behind white women's wages," more than triple Black women's wage disadvantage in the mid-1970s.[58] This estimate, however, actually underestimates the extent of wage inequality since it focuses on women who are employed. Black women suffer from high rates of unemployment even when the rates for other groups are relatively low. In 1999, for instance, 10 percent of

Black women were unemployed, which was double the rate for White women.[59] Further, they are particularly vulnerable to the effects of a recession regardless of what jobs they have or what industry they work in.[60] For example, when unemployed Black women reenter the labor force, the wages employers offer are significantly lower than the wages women who been employed elsewhere are offered. Pettit and Ewert argue that including an estimate of the jobless generated "race differences in offer wages [*sic*] 11%–17% larger than those observed among employed women.[61]

Scholars have pointed to the increasing importance of Black women's life circumstances, such as the increase in the number of households headed by women, the decline in marriage rates for this population, and Black women's lower levels of education relative to White women, as contributing to wage inequality. But none of these fully account for the difference in wages between Black and White women.[62] A portion of the variation in Black and White women's wages is not explained by the characteristics that statisticians measure for these two groups of workers—education, age, experience, marital status, number of children, industry, and occupation. Again and again, scholars are pointing to the salience of unmeasured characteristics, namely discrimination, as a driving force.[63]

Not only did the wages of Black women fall behind relative to those of White women in 1990, Black women also experienced an absolute decline of more than 7 percent in their mean wage, which decreased from $8.69 to $8.06 per hour.[64] However, the median wage of Black women actually increased slightly (by about 1 percent) over this same period, which points to growth on the lower end of the economic and occupational spectrum for that group.[65] The role of occupational segregation in explaining Black women's declining wages cannot be overstated. In their investigation of the cause of the wage differential of Blacks employed in predominately Black jobs versus Blacks employed in predominately White jobs, sociologists Irene Browne, Cynthia Hewitt, Leann Tigges, and Gary Green found that "predominantly Black jobs are overrepresented within the positions that experienced falling returns to wages [declining earnings] with the restructuring of the U.S. economy—service industries and occupations that require few skills."[66]

More than half of all employed Black women in 2008 were clerical or nonhousehold service workers. While this reflects occupational progress in absolute terms since 1960, the extent of their progress is questionable. Figure 6.1 shows the change in the representation of Black women in clerical jobs. There was a significant increase through 1980. In 1990 the proportion of Black and White women employed as clerical workers was roughly equivalent, thereafter the number of Black women employed slightly outpaces White women. Notably, Black women's increases in clerical work through 1980 were not achieved at the expense of White women during that period. In fact, the representation of White women actually increased as well.

Substantial job growth occurred that facilitated Black women's expansion alongside White women. However, as economist Julieanne Malveaux notes, Black and White women were not found in the same

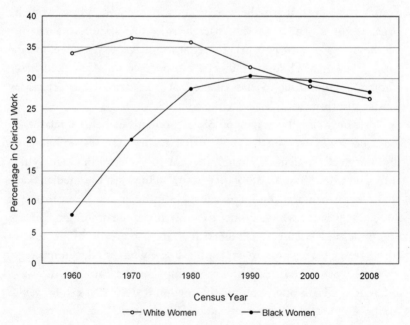

FIGURE 6.1

Proportion of Black and White Women Workers Employed in Clerical and Kindred Occupations, 1960–2008

SOURCE: Author's analysis of data from the Integrated Public Use Microdata Series, Version 5.0.

types of jobs. Black women were overrepresented among the poorly paid clerical occupations such as file clerks or typists.[67] Further, the trend toward the development of large back-office clerical staffs isolated Black women from the general public.[68] Sociologists Evelyn Nakano Glenn and Charles M. Tolbert, II, argue that Black women were "ghettoized within office work ... excluded from jobs that involve greater discretion, contact with the public, and interaction with management."[69]

In addition, clerical work was not the pathway out of poverty that Black women workers had envisioned. The percentage of Black women clerical workers whose income fell at or below the poverty line was nearly 12 percent in 1960, more than double that of White women clerical workers; by 2008, the income of nearly 16 percent of Black women clerical workers was below the poverty line. While Black women clerical workers as a percentage of all Black women workers was equivalent to the corresponding statistic for White women clerical workers in 1990, as Figure 6.2 shows, the poverty rates of these two groups never converged. Black women clerical workers were twice as likely as White women clerical workers to be impoverished.

Black women employed in service work do not fare better. They are concentrated in dead-end, poorly paid, sex-segregated occupations, such as home health care aides.[70] Although the proportion of White female, Black male, and White male workers in nonhousehold service work is growing, the proportion of Black women workers employed in that occupation category widely outpaces those three groups; in 2008, more than 25 percent of Black women workers had such jobs (see Figure 6.3). All groups employed in nonhousehold service face relatively high poverty levels (see Figure 6.4). One of the key reasons Black women remain members of the working poor is that they are overrepresented in these low-wage occupations.

While the economic situation of low-skilled Black women in clerical and service work gives us pause, the situation of skilled Black women in the workplace is equally disheartening. Authority in the workplace is a measure of the extent to which individuals and or groups have been granted legitimate power. While it is true that women traditionally have had less authority than men and Blacks have had less authority than Whites, positions of authority have seemed to bypass Black women altogether.[71]

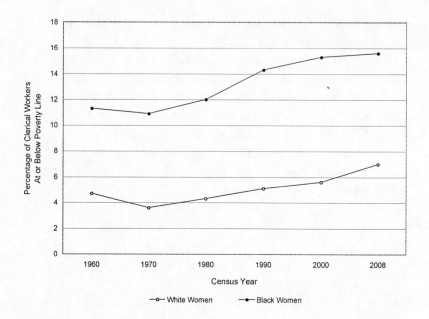

Figure 6.2

Percentage of Black and White Women Clerical and Kindred Workers Whose Incomes Fall at or below the Poverty Line, 1960–2008

Source: Author's analysis of data from the Integrated Public Use Microdata Series, Version 5.0.

Hierarchical relationships of power based on race and gender map directly onto formal authority structures within organizations. Stainback and Tomaskovic-Devey find that White men manage men and women of all races, White women manage women of all races, Black men manage Black men and women, but the only constituency Black women manage is themselves.[72] Thus, Black women are less likely than any other group to be hired for management positions.

Since Black women are perceived to be capable only of managing themselves and they make up such a small proportion of the labor force, the management opportunities open to them will be limited. Black women have made only meager gains in management since 1966, when they were almost completely excluded from that occupational category. Stainback and Tomaskovic-Devey find that although Black women's access to managerial jobs has increased, their levels remain far

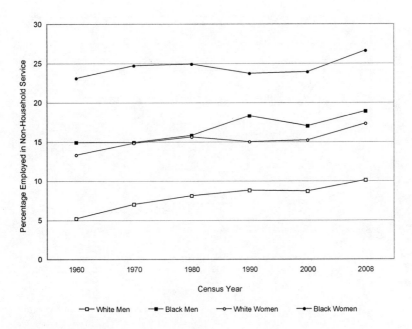

FIGURE 6.3

Distribution of Workers Employed in Nonhousehold Service by Race and Gender, 1960–2008

SOURCE: Author's analysis of data from the Integrated Public Use Microdata Series, Version 5.0.

below their representation in private sector jobs.[73] Further, all of Black women's managerial gains occurred in segregated industrial sectors such as retail, producer services, personal services, and social services; these are some of the fastest-growing sectors in the economy. Without the growth of the low-wage service sector, the meager gains Black women achieved in management would have been even smaller.

No matter what measure of progress we examine—wage equality, occupational distribution, or authority in the workplace—one thing is certain: Black women's quest for definitive progress has been illusory. While they experienced wage gains, they were limited to occupations in which there were shrinking opportunities, namely manufacturing and the public sector. While they substantially increased their representation among clerical workers, that occupation declined as they entered and is now marked by decreasing wages and back-room jobs. Finally,

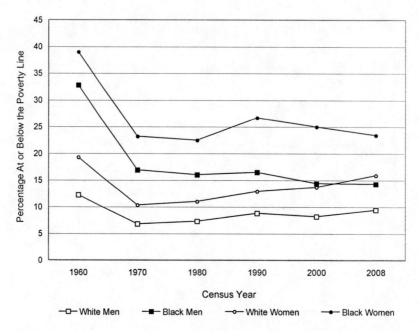

Figure 6.4

Proportion of White Male, Black Male, White Female, and Black Female Workers in Nonhousehold Service Occupations Earning Incomes at or below the Poverty Line, 1960–2008

Source: Author's analysis of data from the Integrated Public Use Microdata Series, Version 5.0.

while Black women have gained access to positions of authority, they are seen fit to manage only other Black women. Hence, while there has been marked improvement in the occupational distribution of Black women since 1960, true progress measured as equitable treatment of Black women in the labor force has surely not been achieved. Although Black women have experienced progress in absolute terms, they are still marginalized in the labor force.

Poor Black Women: A Product of the Intersection of Race, Gender, and Class

A clear connection exists between employer preferences, occupation, and economic class.[74] Employers rank potential employees, whom they see as members of racialized and gendered groups, by preference in the labor queue. Race and gender segregation can be conceived of as the result of the labor queue materialized. In other words, employer preferences, which differentially rank workers, becomes a constraint on occupational achievement, causing employers' preferences to govern reality and determine an individual's likely placement in the occupational structure.

Sociologist Robert L. Kaufman's 2002 study investigated alternative perspectives that explain the allocation of Black and White Workers in jobs, one of which was queuing theory. Within this perspective, employers use race and gender as proxies for productivity, such that "individuals are stereotyped as qualified or not, with more attention given to their membership in a race or gender group and less attention paid to their personal qualifications."[75] In addition, at the level of labor market position, jobs are race- and gender-typed as "stereotypically 'appropriate' or 'inappropriate' for Blacks and women."[76] Kaufman found that when employers do not need workers with particular sets of skills, they hire "their preferred group, White men."[77] Further, jobs that are more desirable that have "sufficient hours, low unemployment, and self-employment" employ more Whites than Blacks and more men than women.[78]

The labor market experiences of Black women exemplify the multidimensional nature of oppression created by race, gender, and class. While race and gender hierarchies are independent systems of power prefaced on the privilege of one group (Whites and males, respectively) and the disadvantage of another (Blacks and females, respectively), they are not parallel hierarchies that create individual oppressions. Instead, as sociologist Patricia Hill Collins argues, social inequality is fundamentally interdependent, resulting from the multiple systems of domination and oppression that structure all of our lives.[79] Placing Black women at the center of my analysis made clear the intersecting, interlocking, and multiplicative nature of race and gender oppression. It illuminated the ways that race and gender disadvantage built on each other in the context of an interlocking structure of power and oppression that dictated where and when Black women could move within the labor market.

When race, gender, and class come together they change each other, sociologist Ivy Ken argues. They "depend on each other for the forms . . . of oppression and privilege they produce because of their coming together."[80] For too long popular discourse has focused on the product of the intersection of race, gender, and class—legions of poor Black women—without examining the structural conditions that produced that result.

Economic class position follows from the unequal distribution of racialized and gendered groups across occupations. Disadvantaged groups are allocated to devalued occupations and receive the "poor working conditions, subservient tasks, low prestige and low pay" associated with them.[81] When privileged groups are found in devalued occupations they are often found in higher-status roles (such as front office versus back-room clerical work) and receive higher wages. Race and gender disadvantage shape earnings—women are routinely paid less than men and Blacks are paid less Whites even when they occupy similar positions. Despite class fracturing along racial and gender lines, all members of the dominant group reap the economic benefits of dominant group position, even if it is not shared equally.

Although we may think of class position as race- and gender-neutral, it is the result of fundamentally racialized and gendered processes. In her book *Class Questions*, sociologist Joan Acker argues that "inequalities are legitimated by gendered and racialized images and understandings, such as the widespread, still existing, image of the manager as a white male with certain characteristics."[82] A similar image based on class and race assumptions is that of an unemployed welfare recipient as a single Black mother. Focusing primarily on work relations, Acker describes the relationships between race, gender, and class as "ongoing processes and practices in which gendering and racialization are integral to the creation and recreation of class inequalities and class divisions."[83] In this volume I have underscored the necessity of an intersectional approach in the study of inequality and have exposed the historical conditions that produced poor, low-skilled Black women and restricted them to devalued segments of the American labor market.

Mary Church Terrell ended her 1904 speech on "The Progress of Colored Women" by saying, "Seeking no favors because of their color nor charity because of their needs they knock at the door of Justice and ask for an equal chance."[84] More than a century later Black women's fight for equality within a racist and sexist society continues. Contrary to popular belief, Black women have not profited in the workplace because of their dual minority status. Instead, they are treading water in the American labor market, struggling to remain afloat, to hold on to meager gains they earned in the 1970s, to gain access to jobs that enable them to exit poverty, and to compete with other groups unencumbered by biases and false perceptions about their ability.

The persistence of high levels of occupational segregation by gender, even as racial segregation has abated, has hindered Black women's progress. They gained access to White women's jobs but failed to advance much farther. Within women's jobs, low-skilled Black women are often segregated yet again, relegated to occupations that are poorly paid, insecure, and have little opportunity for advancement. Educated Black women struggle to advance even though they are highly skilled, and their absence at the roundtables of power symbolically illustrates the persistence of racial and gender inequality and helps perpetuate it.

In many ways, the position of Black women at the back of the labor queue remains unchanged. When they move into new occupations, they gain access to positions no one else wants and are paid wages no other group will accept (except, perhaps, illegal workers). In times of recession and hardship they are unemployed at higher rates and have difficulty recovering. Still among the last hired and first fired, low-skilled Black women labor in a job market hostile to workers without higher education while educated Black women are afforded only a conditional welcome in professional and managerial jobs and are routinely excluded from positions of power. For the majority of Black women, the story of the post–civil rights era is that the struggle for equality continues.

Appendix

Table A.1

Coefficients from Multilevel Analysis of the Influence of Race and Gender on the Occupational Income Score

	Model 1[a]		Model 2[b]		Model 3[c]	
	Co-efficient[d]	Standard Error	Standard Error	Co-efficient	Co-efficient	Standard Error
Level 1 coefficients						
Black	-5.325	0.221			-3.037	0.266
Women			-7.627	0.106	-6.356	0.108
Black women					-2.505	0.458
Age	0.041	0.000	0.040	0.000	0.038	0.000
Married	4.111	0.014	3.186	0.014	3.148	0.014
Number of children	-0.140	0.004	-0.210	0.004	-0.198	0.004
Literate	2.220	0.018	3.231	0.017	2.332	0.018
Urban	3.961	0.013	4.039	0.013	4.172	0.013
Level 2: fixed effects						
North	1.008	0.332	2.733	0.418	1.713	0.353
Midwest	-0.163	0.294	1.059	0.371	0.073	0.312
West	0.412	0.283	1.711	0.354	0.733	0.300
1870	0.019	0.049	-0.647	0.050	-0.207	0.052
1880	-0.081	0.047	-2.146	0.050	-2.017	0.050
1900	-1.042	0.044	-1.212	0.046	-0.944	0.047
1910	-0.530	0.049	-0.586	0.052	-0.262	0.052
1920	0.201	0.043	-0.211	0.045	0.170	0.045
1930	0.468	0.053	0.094	0.056	0.614	0.057
1940	0.291	0.042	0.102	0.046	0.460	0.045
1950	2.632	0.043	3.302	0.046	3.165	0.046
1960	1.723	0.042	2.402	0.045	2.829	0.045
Level 2: random effect						
Intercept	0.541	0.114	0.862	0.182	0.614	0.128
Cross-level interactions						
Black North	-0.559	0.057			-0.805	0.070
Black Midwest	1.053	0.057			0.793	0.067
Black West	-0.274	0.113			-0.820	0.136
Black 1870	0.404	0.229			-1.169	0.276
Black 1880	1.330	0.232			0.024	0.279
Black 1900	0.593	0.227			-0.516	0.274
Black 1910	-1.627	0.236			-1.803	0.285
Black 1920	-2.080	0.226			-2.172	0.121
Black 1930	-2.622	0.242			-2.734	0.291
Black 1940	-2.182	0.224			-2.336	0.291
Black 1950	-1.626	0.223			-2.612	0.269
Black 1960	-1.799	0.224			-2.795	0.270

TABLE A.1 *(continued)*

Coefficients from Multilevel Analysis of the Influence of Race and Gender on the Occupational Income Score

	Model 1[a]		Model 2[b]		Model 3[c]	
	Co-efficient[d]	Standard Error	Standard Error	Co-efficient	Co-efficient	Standard Error
Women North			-1.043	0.033	-2.560	0.037
Women Midwest			0.151	0.034	-1.394	0.038
Women West			-0.371	0.049	-2.004	0.051
Women 1870			1.129	0.127	-0.011	0.113
Women 1880			2.672	0.125	2.557	0.132
Women 1900			2.750	0.114	3.125	0.118
Women 1910			1.888	0.123	2.706	0.128
Women 1920			3.559	0.111	4.575	0.113
Women 1930			2.873	0.130	4.049	0.135
Women 1940			3.545	0.108	4.425	0.110
Women 1950			3.298	0.107	3.838	0.109
Women 1960			2.348	0.107	2.651	0.108
Black Women North					1.700	0.115
Black Women Midwest					0.382	0.120
Black Women West					1.893	0.233
Black Women 1870					5.020	0.481
Black Women 1880					2.475	0.485
Black Women 1900					0.807	0.473
Black Women 1910					-0.646	0.490
Black Women 1920					-3.347	0.470
Black Women 1930					-2.973	0.503
Black Women 1940					-3.187	0.465
Black Women 1950					-1.242	0.463
Black Women 1960					-0.341	0.463
Constant	14.835	0.184	14.096	0.230	15.714	0.196
N	2,982,799		2,982,799		2,982,799	
-2LL[e]	21,989,709		21,965,601		21,853,357	

SOURCE: Author's analysis of data from the Integrated Public Use Microdata Series, Version 5.0.

[a] Model 1 examined race (Black and White workers).
[b] Model 2 examined gender (men and women).
[c] Model 3 examined the interaction of race and gender.
[d] Coefficients are significant if they are twice their standard error at the conventional p < .05 level. Most coefficients are significant at much lower probabilities.
[e] The models presented were selected using the likelihood ratio test. They were shown to be a significant improvement on the null model and earlier models that added the independent variable seen in the final models in succession.

Appendix

TABLE A.2

Distribution of Labor Force Participants by Race and Gender (by percent) and Male-to-Female Ratio by Race, 1860–1960

Year	Men	Women	M/F Ratio	White Men	White Women	White M/F Ratio	Black Men	Black Women	Black M/F Ratio
1860[a]	85.7	14.3	6.0	84.4	13.7	6.2	1.3	0.6	2.0
1870	86.1	13.9	6.2	77.0	4.2	7.9	9.0	4.2	2.2
1880	85.2	14.8	5.8	76.7	10.8	7.1	8.5	4.0	2.1
1900	82.2	17.8	4.6	73.5	13.8	5.3	8.6	4.0	2.1
1910	79.7	20.3	3.9	73.2	16.3	4.5	6.4	4.0	1.6
1920	79.9	20.1	4.0	73.3	17.0	4.3	6.6	3.0	2.2
1930	78.1	21.9	3.6	70.5	18.1	3.9	7.6	3.8	2.0
1940	75.9	24.1	3.1	69.2	20.7	3.3	6.7	3.4	2.0
1950	72.6	27.4	2.6	66.2	24.0	2.8	6.4	3.4	1.9
1960	68.2	31.8	2.1	62.5	28.1	2.3	5.7	3.7	1.5

SOURCE: Author's analysis of data from the Integrated Public Use Microdata Series, Version 5.0.

NOTE: Case selection was based on four factors: 1) age—only individuals 16 years old or older are included; 2) OCCSCORE—only individuals with a valid OCCSCORE value (i.e., not equal to 0) in the IPUMS database are included; 3) labor force status—individuals must have identified themselves as participants in the labor force to census takers; and 4) race—only individuals that identified as Black or White are included in this analysis.

[a] Only Blacks who were free prior to emancipation are included in data for 1860.

Table A.3

Distribution of White Men, Black Men, White Women, and Black Women across Occupational Categories, 1960 (by percent)
(Proportion of group employed in each occupation in parentheses)

Occupation	White Men	Black Men	White Women	Black Women
Professionals & technical workers	60.3 (10.6)	1.6 (3.1)	35.6 (14.2)	2.5 (7.3)
Managers, officials, & proprietors	84.3 (11.2)	1.1 (1.6)	14.1 (4.2)	0.5 (1.1)
Clerical & kindred workers	30.1 (7.0)	2.1 (5.3)	65.8 (34.0)	2.0 (7.9)
Sales workers	62.2 (7.2)	1.0 (1.3)	36.0 (9.2)	0.8 (1.6)
Craftsmen	92.8 (24.8)	4.6 (13.4)	2.5 (1.5)	0.2 (0.9)
Operatives	64.4 (20.1)	7.5 (25.9)	25.3 (17.6)	2.8 (14.5)
Service workers (household)	1.5 (0.1)	1.7 (0.8)	42.2 (4.0)	54.6 (38.5)
Service workers (nonhousehold)	37.4 (5.2)	9.7 (14.9)	43.0 (13.3)	9.9 (23.1)
Farm laborers	79.8 (7.7)	10.7 (11.3)	7.1 (1.5)	2.5 (4.0)
Laborers	72.0 (6.0)	24.3 (22.4)	2.8 (0.5)	0.8 (1.2)

SOURCE: Author's analysis of data from the Integrated Public Use Microdata Series, Version 5.0

Table A,4

Distribution of White Men, Black Men, White Women, and Black Women across Occupational Categories, 1970 (by percent)
(Proportion of group employed in each occupation in parentheses)

Occupation	White Men	Black Men	White Women	Black Women
Professionals & technical workers	57.3 (14.8)	2.1 (5.7)	37.1 (16.6)	3.6 (12.0)
Managers, officials, & proprietors	82.3 (10.8)	1.7 (2.4)	15.4 (3.5)	0.7 (1.1)
Clerical & kindred workers	23.3 (7.1)	2.4 (7.5)	69.3 (36.5)	5.1 (20.1)
Sales workers	58.6 (7.2)	1.5 (1.9)	38.3 (8.1)	1.7 (2.6)
Craftsmen	88.9 (24.6)	6.5 (18.7)	4.2 (2.0)	0.4 (1.5)
Operatives	59.8 (18.6)	8.8 (28.7)	27.2 (14.7)	4.3 (17.2)
Service workers (household)	1.5 (0.0)	1.5 (0.4)	45.4 (2.1)	51.5 (17.7)
Service workers (nonhousehold)	37.2 (7.0)	7.5 (14.9)	45.2 (14.8)	10.1 (24.7)
Farm laborers	81.5 (4.3)	7.9 (4.3)	8.5 (0.8)	2.2 (1.5)
Laborers	73.5 (5.7)	18.9 (15.5)	6.5 (0.9)	1.5 (1.5)

Source: Author's analysis of data from the Integrated Public Use Microdata Series, Version 5.0.

TABLE A.5

Distribution of White Men, Black Men, White Women, and Black Women across Occupational Categories, 1980 (by percent)
(Proportion of group employed in each occupation in parentheses)

Occupation	White Men	Black Men	White Women	Black Women
Professional & technical workers	51.2 (16.2)	2.9 (8.9)	41.2 (18.5)	4.7 (15.2)
Managers, officials, & proprietors	71.1 (13.6)	2.6 (4.8)	24.7 (6.7)	1.6 (3.2)
Clerical & kindred workers	18.6 (6.6)	2.6 (8.9)	71.0 (35.8)	7.8 (28.3)
Sales workers	53.8 (6.8)	2.0 (2.3)	41.8 (7.5)	2.5 (3.2)
Craftsmen	85.3 (22.4)	7.6 (19.3)	6.2 (2.3)	0.9 (2.5)
Operatives	58.9 (16.7)	9.4 (25.8)	26.4 (10.6)	5.3 (15.5)
Service workers (household)	2.6 (0.0)	1.7 (0.2)	53.9 (0.9)	41.8 (4.9)
Service workers (nonhousehold)	34.9 (8.1)	7.1 (15.8)	47.5 (15.6)	10.5 (24.9)
Farm laborers	80.0 (3.2)	4.9 (1.9)	13.9 (0.8)	1.2 (0.5)
Laborers	72.9 (6.3)	14.3 (12.0)	10.6 (1.3)	2.3 (2.0)

SOURCE: Author's analysis of data from the Integrated Public Use Microdata Series, Version 5.0.

TABLE A.6

Distribution of White Men, Black Men, White Women, and Black Women across Occupational Categories, 2008

(Proportion of group employed in each occupation in parentheses)

Occupation	White Men	Black Men	White Women	Black Women
Professionals & technical workers	39.4 (19.6)	3.7 (14.1)	50.3 (29.3)	6.7 (22.4)
Managers, officials, & proprietors	57.2 (17.8)	4.0 (9.6)	34.6 (12.7)	4.3 (9.0)
Clerical & kindred workers	19.1 (7.0)	4.3 (11.8)	64.2 (26.7)	11.6 (27.8)
Sales workers	49.5 (7.2)	4.2 (4.8)	40.9 (7.0)	5.4 (5.3)
Craftsmen	84.7 (17.5)	8.2 (13.2)	6.0 (1.4)	1.2 (1.6)
Operatives	64.3 (12.2)	12.1 (17.9)	18.9 (4.2)	4.7 (6.1)
Service workers (household)	—[a]	—[a]	—[a]	—[a]
Service workers (nonhousehold)	32.3 (10.1)	7.8 (18.9)	47.3 (17.3)	12.6 (26.6)
Farm laborers	77.1 (1.7)	3.0 (0.5)	19.0 (0.5)	0.8 (0.1)
Laborers	76.2 (7.0)	13.0 (9.3)	9.0 (1.0)	1.9 (1.2)

SOURCE: Author's analysis of data from the Integrated Public Use Microdata Series, Version 5.0.

[a] Undefined value because there were no white men in household domestic service in this census year.

NOTES

INTRODUCTION

1. Sociologists Kathryn Edin and Laura Lein found "remarkable dedication to the work ethic" among most of the welfare recipients they interviewed. They "recognized the stigma that their friends, communities, and the larger society imposed on welfare recipients, as well as the boost in self-esteem and social standing they gained from working. This is why they had tried to live off of work in the past and also why they were trying to find work in the future." Kathryn Edin and Laura Lein, "Work, Welfare, and Single Mothers' Economic Survival Strategies," *American Sociological Review* 62 (1997): 263.

2. I use census data on race, gender, and occupational position drawn from the Integrated Public Use Microdata Series (IPUMS). Census data provides the most comprehensive set of quantitative information on long-term changes in the U.S. population. IPUMS integrates the census data samples across years to allow for uniformity in concepts and measures, permitting an analysis of historical change. The measure of occupation that I employ uses 1950 as the standard due to its similarity to the years both before and after, which provides comparability between occupational data across all years studied and greater confidence in the change observed. See Steven Ruggles, J. Trent Alexander, Katie Genadek, Ronald Goeken, Matthew B. Schroeder, and Matthew Sobek, *Integrated Public Use Microdata Series: Version 5.0.* Machine-readable database. (Minneapolis: University of Minnesota, 2010), http://usa.ipums.org/usa/.

3. See Joya Misra, Stephanie Moller, and Marina Karides, "Envisioning Dependency: Changing Media Depictions of Welfare in the 20th Century," *Social Problems* 50, no. 4 (2003): 482–504.

4. See Ivy Kennelly, "'That Single-Mother Element': How White Employers Typify Black Women," *Gender & Society* 13 no. 2 (1999): 168–192.

5. See Phillip Moss and Chris Tilly, *Stories Employers Tell: Race, Skill, and Hiring in America* (New York: Russell Sage Foundation, 2003).

CHAPTER 1.   HIERARCHIES OF PREFERENCE AT WORK

1. W.E.B. Du Bois, *The Souls of Black Folk* (New York: New American Library, 1903), 19.

2. Mary Church Terrell, "The Progress of Colored Women," in *Let Nobody Turn Us Around: Voices of Resistance, Reform, and Renewal, An African American Anthology*, ed. Manning Marable and Leith Mullings (Lanham, Md.: Rowman & Littlefield, 2000), 173.

3. Robert Blauner, *Still the Big News: Racial Oppression in America* (Philadelphia, Pa.: Temple University Press, 2001), 29.

4. Cynthia Fuchs Epstein, *Deceptive Distinctions: Sex, Gender, and the Social Order* (New York: Russell Sage Foundation, 1988), 6.
5. R. W. Connell, *Gender and Power* (Oxford: Polity Press, 1987), 99.
6. Evelyn Nakano Glenn, "From Servitude to Service Work: Historical Continuities in the Racial Division of Paid Reproductive Labor," *Signs* 18 (1992): 2.
7. Ibid., 7.
8. Chinese men in the West provide an important exception to the designation of laundry work as women's work exclusively. However, their performance of this work was a result of the shortage of women and their marginalized status within the labor market. Historian Joan S. Wang found that "due to their non-citizen status, the closed labor market, and the shortage of women, Chinese males substituted to some extent for female labor in the American West." Joan S. Wang, "Race, Gender and Laundry Work: The Roles of Chinese Laundrymen and American Women in the United States, 1850–1950," *Journal of American Ethnic History* 20 no. 1 (2004): 60.
9. Jacqueline Jones, *Labor of Love, Labor of Sorrow: Black Women, Work, and the Family, from Slavery to the Present* (New York: Vintage Books, 1986), 178.
10. Ibid., 261.
11. See ibid., 196–231, chapter on the Great Depression.
12. Maxine Baca Zinn and Bonnie Thornton Dill, "Theorizing Difference from Multiracial Feminism," *Feminist Studies* 22 (Summer 1996): 327.
13. Aida Hurtado, "Relating to Privilege: Seduction and Rejection in the Subordination of White Women and Women of Color," *Signs* 14 (1989): 854.
14. bell hooks, "Racism and Feminism," in *Theories of Race and Racism: A Reader*, ed. Les Back and John Solomos (New York: Routledge, 2000), 375.
15. Gloria T. Hull, Patricia Bell Scott, and Barbara Smith, eds., *All of the Women Are White, All Blacks Are Men, But Some of Us Are Brave* (Old Westbury, N.Y.: Feminist Press, 1982).
16. Judith Lorber, *Gender Inequality: Feminist Theories and Politics* (Los Angeles: Roxbury Publishing Company, 2005), 196.
17. Irene Browne and Joya Misra, "The Intersection of Gender and Race in the Labor Market," *Annual Review of Sociology* 29 (2003): 489.
18. Deborah King, "Multiple Jeopardy, Multiple Consciousness: The Context of Black Feminist Ideology," *Signs* 14 (1988).
19. Patricia Hill Collins, *Black Feminist Thought: Knowledge, Consciousness, and the Politics of Empowerment* (New York: Routledge, 2000), 18.
20. Ibid.
21. Browne and Misra, "The Intersection of Gender and Race in the Labor Market," 491.
22. Ibid., 492.
23. Integrated Public Use Microdata Series (IPUMS) data permits analysis of economic differences that are occupationally based. Prior to 1940, the census did not collect income information, so it is not possible to directly measure individual differences in income for the vast majority of the period I am studying. IPUMS designers have constructed a variable that assigns an occupational income score (a value approximating the median total income—in hundreds of 1950 dollars—for all individuals employed in a particular occupation) to each of the 970 occupations identified in 1950. The strength of this variable is that it standardizes income across time. The occupational income score does not include a measure of prestige and is free from the subjective bias that characterizes the widely used Duncan socioeconomic index

that is attributable to changes over time in how occupations were valued. Indeed, in reviewing the vast literature on objective and subjective measures of occupational status, historian Matthew Sobek concludes that "most of what prestige measurement captures is, in any case, economic standing. An objective score like income presents fewer interpretive problems." Matthew Sobek, "The Comparability of Occupations and the Generation of Income Scores," *Historical Methods* 28 (Winter 1995): 50.

24. Barbara Reskin and Camille Z. Charles, "Now You See 'Em, Now You Don't: Race, Ethnicity, and Gender in Labor Market Research," in *African-American and Latina Women at Work*, ed. Irene Browne (New York: Russell Sage Foundation, 1999).

25. Browne and Misra, "The Intersection of Gender and Race in the Labor Market," 490.

26. Frances Beale, "Double Jeopardy: To Be Black and Female," in *The Black Woman: An Anthology*, ed. Toni Cade [Bambara] (New York: Signet, 1970), 95.

27. Lorber, *Gender Inequality*, 196.

28. Eduardo Bonilla-Silva, "Rethinking Racism: Toward a Structural Interpretation," *American Sociological Review* 62 no. 3 (1996): 469.

29. Blauner, *Still the Big News*, 26.

30. Myra H. Strober and Carolyn L. Arnold, "The Dynamics of Occupational Segregation among Bank Tellers," in *Gender in the Workplace*, ed. Clair Brown and Joseph Pechman (Washington, D.C.: Brookings Institution, 1987), 107–148.

31. Evelyn Nakano Glenn, "Racial Ethnic Women's Labor: The Intersection of Race, Gender, and Class Oppression," in *Gender, Family, and Economy: The Triple Overlap*, ed. Rae Lesser Blumberg (Newbury Park, Calif.: Sage, 1991), 176.

32. Stanley Lieberson, *A Piece of Pie: Blacks and White Immigrants since 1880* (Berkeley: University of California Press, 1980), 296.

33. Charles Tilly, *Durable Inequality* (Berkeley: University of California Press, 1998), 154.

34. Lester Thurow, "Education and Economic Equality," *Public Interest* 28 (Summer 1972): 73.

35. Barbara F. Reskin and Patricia Roos, *Job Queues, Gender Queues* (Philadelphia, Pa.: Temple University Press, 1992), 34.

36. I use the term employers' preferences here for continuity rather than rankers' preferences, which Reskin and Roos used in their original formulation in *Job Queues, Gender Queues*.

37. William A. Darity, Jr., and Patrick L. Mason, "Evidence of Discrimination in Employment: Codes of Color, Codes of Gender," *Journal of Economic Perspectives* 12, no. 2 (1998): 64.

38. Ibid., 65.

39. Peter M. Blau and Otis D. Duncan, *The American Occupational Structure* (New York: John Wiley & Sons, 1967), 207.

CHAPTER 2. AS GOOD AS ANY MAN

1. See George M. Frederickson, *Racism: A Short History* (Princeton, N.J.: Princeton University Press, 2002), 30–39, for an expansive discussion of the enslavement of Europeans, Native Americans, Asians, and Blacks.

2. Adrienne Davis, "Don't Let Nobody Bother Yo' Principle": The Sexual Economy of Slavery," in *Sister Circle: Black Women and Work*, ed. Sharon Harley and the Black Women and Work Collectives (New Brunswick, N.J.: Rutgers University Press, 2002), 107.

3. Davis, "Don't Let Nobody Bother Yo' Principle," 106.

4. Ibid., 107.

5. Ibid., 106.

6. Manning Marable, Nishani Frazier, and John Campbell McMillian, *Freedom on My Mind: The Columbia Documentary History of the African American Experience* (New York: Columbia University Press, 2003), 512.

7. Davis, "Don't Let Nobody Bother Yo' Principle," 109.

8. Dorothy Roberts, *Killing the Black Body: Race, Reproduction, and the Meaning of Liberty* (New York: Pantheon Books, 1997), 39.

9. Ibid.

10. Frederickson, *Racism*, 30–31.

11. Jacqueline Jones, *Labor of Love, Labor of Sorrow: Black Women, Work, and the Family, from Slavery to the Present* (New York: Vintage Books, 1986), 16.

12. For further discussion of this see the example of Rose Williams in Roberts, *Killing the Black Body*, 22.

13. James Oliver Horton, "Freedom's Yoke: Gender Conventions among Antebellum Free Blacks," *Feminist Studies* 12, no. 1 (1986): 53.

14. Robert Blauner, *Still the Big News: Racial Oppression in America* (Philadelphia, Pa.: Temple University Press, 2001), 50.

15. Frederickson, *Racism*, 54.

16. Ibid., 64.

17. Ibid., 79.

18. James Henry Hammond, *Selections from the Letters and Speeches of the Hon. James H. Hammond; of South Carolina* (New York: John F. Trow & Co., 1866), 318.

19. Abraham Lincoln and Stephen Arnold Douglas, *Political Debates between Abraham Lincoln and Stephen A. Douglas in the Celebrated Campaign of 1858 in Illinois: Including the Preceding Speeches of Each at Chicago, Springfield, Etc., Also the Two Great Speeches of Abraham Lincoln in Ohio in 1859* (Cleveland, Ohio: Burrows Bros. Co., 1894), 164.

20. Blauner, *Still the Big News*, 30.

21. Ibid., 32.

22. Deborah Gray White, *Ar'n't I a Woman?: Female Slaves in the Plantation South* (New York: W. W. Norton, 1999), 165.

23. Jones, *Labor of Love*, 52.

24. White, *Ar'n't I a Woman?*, 169.

25. Ibid.

26. Eric Foner, *Reconstruction: America's Unfinished Revolution 1863–1877* (New York: Harper & Row, 1988), 154.

27. Ibid.

28. Jones, *Labor of Love*, 52.

29. Foner, *Reconstruction*, 200.

30. Evelyn Nakano Glenn, *Unequal Freedom: How Race and Gender Shaped American Citizenship and Labor* (Cambridge, Mass.: Harvard University Press, 2002), 90, italics in original.

31. David Eugene Conrad, *The Forgotten Farmers: The Story of Sharecroppers in the New Deal* (Urbana, Ill.: University of Illinois Press, 1965), 5.
32. Foner, *Reconstruction*, 157.
33. Ibid., 144.
34. Ibid., 143–144.
35. Ibid., 132.
36. For further discussion of this, see ibid., 132–133.
37. Ibid., 139–140.
38. See Jones, *Labor of Love*, 58–60.
39. Ibid., 45.
40. Faye E. Dudden, *Serving Women: Household Service in Nineteenth-Century America* (Middletown, Conn.: Wesleyan University Press, 1983), 13.
41. Jones, *Labor of Love*, 59.
42. Herbert G. Gutman, *The Black Family in Slavery and Freedom, 1750–1925* (New York: Pantheon Books, 1976), 167.
43. Ibid., 168.
44. Ibid.
45. White, *Ar'n't I a Woman?*, 180.
46. Ibid., 173–174.
47. Ibid. 174.
48. Jones, *Labor of Love*, 55.
49. Ibid.
50. Solomon Northup, "Daily Life of Plantation Slaves," in *Black Women in White America: A Documentary History*, ed. Gerda Lerner (New York: Vintage Books, 1992), 15.
51. Jones, *Labor of Love*, 55.
52. Foner, *Reconstruction*, 128.
53. Ibid., 132.
54. Gutman, *The Black Family*, 166.
55. Foner, *Reconstruction*, 134.
56. See ibid., 134–135.
57. Gutman, *The Black Family*, 166.
58. Ibid.
59. Foner, *Reconstruction*, 129.
60. Ibid., 131.
61. Ibid., 155.
62. Ibid., 156.
63. Ibid.
64. Ibid.
65. Ibid., 133.
66. Ibid.
67. Ibid., 134.
68. Ibid.
69. Ibid., 133.
70. Ibid., 158.
71. Major General William T. Sherman, Special Field Orders, No. 15, January 16, 1865, Headquarters Military Division of the Mississippi, Orders & Circulars, series 44, Adjutant General's Office, Record Group 94, National Archives and Records Administration, Washington, D.C.
72. Foner, *Reconstruction*, 159.

73. Ibid.
74. For a detailed discussion of General Sherman's Special Field Orders, No. 15, Howard Circular 13 and 15, and President Johnson's special pardons restoring property to former confederates, see ibid., 158–164.
75. Foner, *Reconstruction*, 160.
76. Ibid., 161.
77. Ibid., 165.
78. Ibid., 166.
79. Glenn, *Unequal Freedom*, 70.
80. Jones, *Labor of Love*, 62.
81. Gutman, *The Black Family*, 167.
82. White, *Ar'n't I a Woman?*, 182.
83. See Foner, *Reconstruction*, 138–139.
84. Ibid., 139.
85. Ibid., 173.
86. See ibid., 140–142.
87. Gutman, *The Black Family*, 168, italics in original.
88. William H. Chafe, Raymond Gavins, and Robert Korstad, *Remembering Jim Crow: African Americans Tell About Life in the Segregated South* (New York: The New Press, 2001), 205.
89. Jones, *Labor of Love*, 58–59.
90. White, *Ar'n't I a Woman?*, 182.
91. Ibid.
92. Glenn, *Unequal Freedom*, 102.
93. Ibid., 87.
94. Ibid., 103.
95. Jones, *Labor of Love*, 46.
96. Glenn, *Unequal Freedom*, 100.
97. For a list of the variables enumerators were required to collect for the 1870 census, see http://usa.ipums.org/usa/voliii/items1870.shtml#desc.
98. Glenn, *Unequal Freedom*, 101.
99. Ibid.
100. For further discussion of this, see Margo Anderson Conk, "Occupational Classification in the United States Census: 1870–1940," *Journal of Interdisciplinary History* 9, no. 1 (1978): 111–130; and Margo Anderson Conk, "Accuracy, Efficiency, and Bias: The Interpretation of Women's Work in the U.S. Census of Occupations, 1890–1940," *Historical Methods* 14 (1981): 65–72.
101. Collected from the folk tradition by Colonial Williamsburg in 1960; see http://www.history.org/history/teaching/enewsletter/february03/work-songs.cfm.
102. Jones, *Labor of Love*, 58.
103. Elaine Ellis, "Women of the Cotton Fields," in *Let Nobody Turn Us Around: Voices of Resistance, Reform, and Renewal, An African American Anthology*, ed. Manning Marable and Leith Mullings (Lanham, Md.: Rowman & Littlefield, 2000), 326.
104. Jones, *Labor of Love*, 260.
105. Mamie E. Locke, "From Three-Fifths to Zero: Implications of the Constitution for African-American Women, 1787–1870," in *"We Specialize in the Wholly Impossible": A Reader in Black Woman's History*, ed. Darlene Clark Hines (Brooklyn, N.Y.: Carlson Publishing, 1995), 226.

106. Bart Landry, *Black Working Wives: Pioneers of the American Family Revolution* (Berkeley: University of California Press, 2000), 42.
107. Glenn, *Unequal Freedom*, 103.
108. Ibid.

CHAPTER 3. EXCELLENT SERVANTS

1. Angela Y. Davis, *Women, Race, & Class* (New York: Vintage Books, 1983), 5.
2. Asian men in the West are an important exception to this rule because of the unbalanced sex ratio there in the nineteenth century. Historian David M. Katzman observes that "in 1880, California and Washington were the only states in which a majority of domestic servants were men." David M. Katzman, *Seven Days a Week: Women and Domestic Service in Industrializing America* (New York: Oxford University Press, 1978), 55. Historian Joan S. Wang speculates that this situation was the result of the "distance from the ports of entry of European immigrants and from Black servants in the South." Joan S. Wang, "Race, Gender, and Laundry Work: The Roles of Chinese Laundrymen and American Women in the United States, 1850–1950," *Journal of American Ethnic History* 20, no. 1 (2004): 60.
3. Evelyn Nakano Glenn, *Unequal Freedom: How Race and Gender Shaped American Citizenship and Labor* (Cambridge, Mass.: Harvard University Press, 2002), 61–62.
4. Ibid., 62.
5. Charles Mackay, *Life and Liberty in America: Sketches of a Tour in the United States and Canada in 1857–1858* (London: Smith, Elder & Co., 1859), 45–46.
6. Faye E. Dudden, *Serving Women: Household Service in Nineteenth-Century America* (Middletown, Conn.: Wesleyan University Press, 1983), 18.
7. Ibid., 33–34.
8. Evelyn Nakano Glenn, "From Servitude to Service Work: Historical Continuities in the Racial Division of Paid Reproductive Labor," *Signs* 18 (1992): 14.
9. Hasia R. Diner, *Erin's Daughters in America: Irish Immigrant Women in the Nineteenth Century* (Baltimore: Johns Hopkins University Press, 1983), 89.
10. "Domestic Servants," *New York Times*, July 7, 1872.
11. For further discussion of this, see David M. Katzman, *Seven Days a Week: Women and Domestic Service in Industrializing America* (New York: Oxford University Press, 1978), 66.
12. Mary Romero, "Sisterhood and Domestic Service: Race, Class, and Gender in the Mistress-Maid Relationship," *Humanity & Society* 12, no. 4 (1988): 326.
13. Glenn, "From Servitude to Service Work," 8.
14. "Domestic Servants," *New York Times*, July 7, 1872.
15. Ibid.
16. Ibid.
17. Romero, "Sisterhood and Domestic Service," 326.
18. Elizabeth L. O'Leary, *From Morning to Night: Domestic Service at Maymont and the Gilded-Age South* (Charlottesville: University of Virginia Press, 2003), 37.
19. Carole Marks, "The Bone and Sinew of the Race: Black Women, Domestic Service and Labor Migration," *Marriage and Family Review* 19 (1993): 161.

20. Bart Landry, *Black Working Wives: Pioneers of the American Family Revolution* (Berkeley: University of California Press, 2000), 49.
21. Katzman, *Seven Days a Week*, 48, 72.
22. O'Leary, *From Morning to Night*.
23. See Katzman, *Seven Days a Week*, 48, 67–70.
24. Romero, "Sisterhood and Domestic Service," 326.
25. For further discussion of racism and deference, see Judith Rollins, *Between Women: Domestics and Their Employers* (Philadelphia, Pa.: Temple University Press, 1985), 200–203.
26. Tera W. Hunter, "Domination and Resistance: The Politics of Wage House-hold Labor in New South Atlanta," in *"We Specialize in the Wholly Impossible": A Reader in Black Woman's History*, ed. Darlene Clark Hines (Brooklyn, N.Y.: Carlson Publishing, 1995), 345.
27. Ibid.
28. Ibid., 346.
29. Ibid., 350.
30. Ibid.
31. O'Leary, *From Morning to Night*, 84.
32. Glenn, "From Servitude to Service Work," 13.
33. Jacqueline Jones, *Labor of Love, Labor of Sorrow: Black Women, Work, and the Family, from Slavery to the Present* (New York: Vintage Books, 1986), 220.
34. For further discussion of the racial and sexual politics of federal public works projects, see ibid., 216–221.
35. Ibid., 220.
36. Julia Kirk Blackwelder, "Women in the Work Force: Atlanta, New Orleans, and San Antonio, 1930–1940," *Journal of Urban History* 4, no. 2 (May 1978): 355.
37. St. Clair Drake and Horace R. Clayton, *Black Metropolis: A Study of Negro Life in a Northern City* (New York: Harper & Row, 1962), 246.
38. O'Leary, *From Morning to Night*, 82.
39. "Even if black women had had white women's characteristics . . . over 50% of black women would have been domestic servants." James S. Cunningham and Nadja Zalokar, "The Economic Progress of Black Women, 1940–1980: Occupational Distribution and Relative Wages," *Industrial and Labor Relations Review* 45, no. 3 (1992): 550.
40. Laurie B. Green, "'Where Would the Negro Women Apply for Work?': Gender, Race, and Labor in Wartime Memphis," *Labor: Studies in Working-Class History of the Americas* 3, no. 3 (2006): 96.
41. Ibid., 97.
42. Ibid.
43. Jones, *Labor of Love*, 237.
44. Ibid.
45. Lorenzo J. Greene and Myra Colson Callis, *The Employment of Negroes in the District of Columbia* (Washington, D.C.: The Association for the Study of Negro Life and History, Inc., 1936), Box 193–40, Folder 8, Myra Colson Callis Papers, Moorland Spingarn Research Center, Howard University, Washington, D.C.
46. Callis and Greene, "The Employment of Negroes," 76.
47. Excerpt from "Domestic Service," *New York Times*, July 7, 1872.
48. Callis and Greene, "The Employment of Negroes," 75.

49. Ibid.
50. C. Douglas Sager to District of Columbia Employment Center, October 3, 1939, Box 193–42, Folder 8, Myra Colson Callis Papers, Moorland Spingarn Research Center, Howard University, Washington, D.C.
51. After analyzing data on household spending patterns in six cities from 1934 to 1936 (Portland, Maine; Lansing, Michigan; Jackson, Mississippi; Indianapolis, Indiana; Denver, Colorado; and Los Angeles, California), Phyllis Palmer writes "A scrutiny of women in this lower-middle-class group indicates the depth of middle-class reliance on domestic service and reveals how central domestic labor was to a household's self-definition as middle class. Moreover, the data point up a truth often hinted at in the 1930s—any woman with enough income would manage to hire some of her work done." Further, "in the South, where severe racial discrimination limited black women to domestic work, only 19 percent of Jackson's white households did not hire some household labor." Phyllis Palmer, *Domesticity and Dirt: Housewives and Domestic Servants in the United States, 1920–1945* (Philadelphia, Pa.: Temple University Press, 1989), 8–9.
52. Callis and Greene, "The Employment of Negroes," 83.
53. Ibid., 84.
54. Mary Anderson, "An Occupational Analysis of Household Employment," 1938, Box 193–45, Folder 2, Myra Colson Callis Papers, Moorland Spingarn Research Center, Howard University, Washington, D.C.
55. Ruth B. Greig to District of Columbia Employment Center, August 23, 1940, Box 193–42, Folder 7, Myra Colson Callis Papers, Moorland Spingarn Research Center, Howard University, Washington, D.C.

CHAPTER 4. EXISTING ON THE INDUSTRIAL FRINGE

1. Skilled and semi-skilled laborers are captured in the census under the category of craftsmen. In addition to traditional skilled laborers, such as blacksmiths, carpenters, etc., this category also includes foremen, machinists, and other craftsmen and kindred workers. This group of workers was most often associated with factory work.
2. Verification procedures used by the census bureau from 1890 to 1940 reexamined information cards submitted by enumerators looking for inaccuracies related to the occupation variable. Inaccuracies were determined to have occurred when the stated occupation was not congruent with the prevailing ideology about which occupations targeted groups should be employed in. During this period, the groups enumerators looked at closely were Blacks in the North, foreign-born persons in the South, women in men's jobs, and men in women's jobs. See Christine E. Bose, *Women in 1900: Gateway to the Political Economy of the 20th Century* (Philadelphia, Pa.: Temple University Press, 2001), 13.
    Historian Margo Anderson Conk suggests that there was pressure to change the occupations self-reported by the workers to one that was non-controversial, or consistent with prevailing notions, resulting in less precise data. See Margo Anderson Conk, "Accuracy, Efficiency, and Bias: The Interpretation of Women's Work in the U.S. Census of Occupations, 1890–1940," *Historical Methods* 14 (1981): 65–72. Thus, it is possible that the data I present on Black women's work particularly in an undesirable occupation such as

domestic service is inflated due to the widely held perception that this work was suitable for Black women, while Black women's work in a more desirable occupation, such as craftsmen—a male-dominated, skilled occupational category—was undercounted. However, the historical record provided in published and unpublished texts strongly suggests that the concentration of Black women in undesirable jobs was not manufactured by changes to the census code.

Yet the challenge to census reliability cannot be discounted, and it is not possible given the large period under study herein to return to original census records. Thus, I have limited my analysis to broad occupational categories only, rather than delineating within each category. I provide in broad brushstrokes a picture of Black women's work over the century.

3. See the detailed tables in Enobong Hannah Branch, "Between a Rock and a Hard Place: Black Women, a Century in the Bottom Class, 1860–1960" (PhD diss., State University of New York at Albany, 2007).

4. Norris W. Preyer, "The Historian, The Slave, and the Ante-Bellum Textile Industry," *Journal of Negro History* 46, no. 2 (1961): 78.

5. Jacqueline Jones, *Labor of Love, Labor of Sorrow: Black Women, Work, and the Family, from Slavery to the Present* (New York: Vintage Books, 1986), 136.

6. For further discussion, see Dolores Janiewski, "Sisters under Their Skins: Southern Working Women, 1880–1950," in *Black Women in United States History*, vol. 3, ed. Darlene Clark Hine, (Brooklyn, N.Y.: Carlson Publishing, 1990), 789–793.

7. Evelyn Nakano Glenn, "Racial Ethnic Women's Labor: The Intersection of Race, Gender, and Class Oppression," in *Gender, Family, and Economy: The Triple Overlap*, ed. Rae Lesser Blumberg (Newbury Park, Calif.: Sage, 1991), 187.

8. Janiewski, "Sisters under Their Skins," 792.

9. Ibid.

10. Ibid.

11. Beverly W. Jones, "Race, Sex, and Class: Black Female Tobacco Workers in Durham, North Carolina, 1920–1940, and the Development of Female Consciousness," in *Black Women in United States History*, vol. 3, ed. Darlene Clark Hine (Brooklyn, N.Y.: Carlson Publishing, 1990), 808–809.

12. Mary Elizabeth Pidgeon, *Negro Women in Industry in 15 States*, Women's Bureau bulletin no. 70 (Washington, D.C.: Government Printing Office, 1929), 16, Box 193–46, Folder 7, Myra Colson Callis Papers, Moorland Spingarn Research Center, Howard University, Washington, D.C.

13. Jones, "Race, Sex, and Class," 808.

14. Ibid.

15. Pidgeon, *Negro Women in Industry in 15 States*, 16.

16. Jones, "Race, Sex, and Class," 811.

17. Ibid.

18. Ibid., 808.

19. Ibid.

20. Dolores Janiewski "Seeking a 'New Day and a New Way': Black Women and Unions in the Southern Tobacco Industry," in *Black Women in United States History*, vol. 3, ed. Darlene Clark Hine (Brooklyn, N.Y.: Carlson Publishing, 1990), 764.

21. Ibid., 762–763.

22. Ibid., 763.
23. Ibid.
24. Milton C. Sernett, *Bound for the Promised Land: African American Religion and the Great Migration* (Durham, N.C.: Duke University Press, 1997).
25. For a more detailed discussion, see David Roediger, *The Wages of Whiteness: Race and the Making of the American Working Class* (New York: Verso Books, 2007), 133–137.
26. Ibid., 134.
27. Ibid., 150.
28. "Labor agents went South to bring Negro workers, whether employable or nor, to the northern industries, and railways provided free transportation to anyone who was foot-loose and adventurous enough to leave"; Alma Herbst, *The Negro in the Slaughtering and Meat-Packing Industry in Chicago* (Boston: Houghton Mifflin, 1932), xx.
29. Ibid., 18.
30. Ibid., 23.
31. For further discussion, see ibid., 22–27.
32. Ibid., 18.
33. Ibid., 19.
34. Ibid.
35. Ibid., 34.
36. Cliff Brown, "The Role of Employers in Split Labor Markets: An Event-Structure Analysis of Racial Conflict and AFL Organizing, 1917–1919," *Social Forces* 79, no. 2 (2000): 665.
37. Ibid.
38. Ibid., 667.
39. Stanley Lieberson, *A Piece of Pie: Blacks and White Immigrants since 1880* (Berkeley: University of California Press, 1980), 339. Also see Herman D. Bloch, *The Circle of Discrimination* (New York: New York University Press, 1969), chapter 5.
40. Ibid., 344.
41. Herbst, *The Negro in the Slaughtering and Meat-Packing Industry in Chicago*, 2.
42. W.E.B. Du Bois, *The Philadelphia Negro: A Social Study* (New York: Schocken Books, 1996), 332–333. Du Bois pointed out that trade unions would treat foreign workers in a similar way if they could, "but here public opinion within and without their ranks forbids hostile action."
43. Herbst, *The Negro in the Slaughtering and Meat-Packing Industry in Chicago*, 74–75.
44. Ibid., 5–6.
45. Ibid., 76.
46. Ibid., 77–78.
47. Ibid., 76.
48. Ibid., 79.
49. Ibid.
50. Ibid., 76.
51. Ibid.
52. Ibid., 78.
53. Ibid., 77.
54. Ibid.
55. Ibid., 72.

56. Consumers' League of Eastern Pennsylvania, *Colored Women as Industrial Workers in Philadelphia* (Philadelphia, Pa.: Consumers' League of Eastern Pennsylvania, 1920), 7, Box 193–45, Folder 11, Myra Colson Callis Papers, Moorland Spingarn Research Center, Howard University, Washington, D.C.
57. Glenn, "Racial Ethnic Women's Labor," 178.
58. Janiewski, "Sisters under Their Skins," 763.
59. Consumers' League of Eastern Pennsylvania, *Colored Women as Industrial Workers in Philadelphia*, 7.
60. Nelle Swartz, *A New Day for the Colored Woman Worker: A Study of Colored Women in Industry in New York City* (New York: Consumers' League of the City of New York, 1919), 5, Box 193–45, Folder 10, Myra Colson Callis Papers, Moorland Spingarn Research Center, Howard University, Washington, D.C.
61. Consumers' League of Eastern Pennsylvania, *Colored Women as Industrial Workers in Philadelphia*, 8–9.
62. Ibid., 10.
63. Ibid., 8.
64. Swartz,, *A New Day for the Colored Woman Worker*, 17.
65. Consumers' League of Eastern Pennsylvania, *Colored Women as Industrial Workers in Philadelphia*, 27.
66. Ibid., 10.
67. Ibid., 9.
68. Ibid., 28.
69. Ibid., 29.
70. Karen Tucker Anderson, "Last Hired, First Fired: Black Women Workers during World War II," *Journal of American History* 69, no. 1 (1982): 83–84.
71. Ibid., 84.
72. Jones, *Labor of Love*, 238.
73. Anderson, "Last Hired, First Fired," 85.
74. Ibid., 86.
75. Jones, *Labor of Love*, 135.
76. Ibid., 252.
77. Anderson, "Last Hired, First Fired," 86.
78. "Conference on Equal Opportunity," *Monthly Labor Review* 79 (1956): 33.
79. Jones, *Labor of Love*, 178–179.
80. Ibid., 168.
81. "Conference on Equal Opportunity," 33.
82. Ibid.
83. Jones, *Labor of Love*, 252–253.
84. Ibid., 153.
85. Ibid., 53. But employers swiftly reinstituted barriers once the labor shortage ended or the pressure abated. "White employers slowly and grudgingly lowered the barriers against blacks when wartime imperatives and black political pressure left them no choice, but they hastily erected the same barriers at the first sign of peace" (234).
86. Ibid., 238.
87. Ibid.
88. Anderson, "Last Hired, First Fired," 87.
89. Jones, *Labor of Love*, 252.

90. Quoted in Michael Keith Honey, *Black Workers Remember: An Oral History of Segregation, Unionism, and the Freedom Struggle* (Berkeley: University of California Press, 1999), 95–96.
91. Ibid., 98.
92. Ibid., 99.
93. Anderson, "Last Hired, First Fired," 96.
94. For further discussion of this see Honey, *Black Workers Remember*, 150–154.
95. Ibid., 104–105.

CHAPTER 5. YOUR BLUES AIN'T NOTHING LIKE MINE

1. Robert Blauner, *Still the Big News: Racial Oppression in America* (Philadelphia: Temple University Press, 2001), 25.
2. Melvin Oliver and Thomas Shapiro, *Black Wealth/White Wealth: A New Perspective on Racial Inequality* (New York: Routledge, 1995), 5.
3. R. W. Connell, *Gender and Power* (Oxford: Polity Press, 1987), 104.
4. Eduardo Bonilla-Silva, "Rethinking Racism: Toward a Structural Interpretation," *American Sociological Review* 62, no. 3 (1997): 470.
5. Evelyn Nakano Glenn, "From Servitude to Service Work: Historical Continuities in the Racial Division of Paid Reproductive Labor," *Signs* 18 (1992): 34.
6. Jacqueline Jones, *American Work: Four Centuries of Black and White Labor* (New York: W. W. Norton, 1998), 13.
7. For further discussion of this, see Bonilla-Silva, "Rethinking Racism," 470.
8. Gunnar Myrdal, *An American Dilemma*, vols. 1 and 2 (New York: Harper & Row, 1944, 1962), 2:575, quoted in Barbara Reskin, "Sex Segregation in the Workplace," *Annual Review of Sociology* 19 (1993): 242.
9. Stanley Lieberson, *A Piece of Pie: Blacks and White Immigrants since 1880* (Berkeley: University of California Press, 1980), 296.
10. Walter Licht, *Industrializing America: The Nineteenth Century* (Baltimore: John Hopkins University Press, 1995).
11. Scott Coltrane, *Family Man: Fatherhood, Housework, and Gender Equity* (New York: Oxford University Press, 1996), 27.
12. Enobong Hannah Branch, "Between a Rock and a Hard Place: Black Women, a Century in the Bottom Class, 1860–1960" (PhD diss., State University of New York at Albany, 2007).
13. Barbara M. Posada, "Crossing the Collar Line: Working Women at Desks, Switchboards, and Tables," *Journal of Urban History* 23, no. 6 (1997): 778. Posada notes that the criteria of being presentable "generally excluded immigrants as well as persons of color." Also see Carole Marks, "The Bone and Sinew of the Race: Black Women, Domestic Service, and Labor Migration," *Marriage and Family Review* 19 (1993): 164.
14. Jones, *Labor of Love*, 179.
15. Addie W. Hunter, "A Colored Working Girl and Race Prejudice," *Crisis* 6 (April 1916): 32–34, quoted in Jones, *Labor of Love*, 179.
16. Edward William Noland and Edward Wight Bakke, *Workers Wanted: A Study of Employers' Hiring Policies, Preferences and Practices in New Haven and Charlotte* (New York: Harper & Brothers, 1977), 66–67.
17. Jones, *Labor of Love*, 179.
18. Ibid.

19. Julia Kirk Blackwelder, "Women in the Work Force: Atlanta, New Orleans, and San Antonio, 1930–1940," *Journal of Urban History* 4, no. 2 (May 1978): 342.

20. Ibid., 354.

21. Francille Rusan Wilson, " 'All of the Glory . . . Faded . . . Quickly': Sadie T. M. Alexander and Black Professional Women, 1920–1950," in *Sister Circle: Black Women and Work*, ed. Sharon Harley and the Black Women and Work Collectives (New Brunswick: Rutgers University Press, 2002), 166.

22. Quote from oral history interview of Sadie T. M. Alexander by Walter M. Phillips, December 10, 1977, Urban History Archives, Temple University, Philadelphia, quoted in Wilson, "All of the Glory . . . Faded . . . Quickly."

23. Bart Landry, *Black Working Wives: Pioneers of the American Family Revolution* (Berkeley: University of California Press, 2000), 74.

24. Whether an individual was in a poverty-level job was determined using the method designed by Horton, Allen, Herring, and Thomas. See Hayward Derrick Horton, Beverlyn Lundy Allen, Cedric Herring, and Melvin E. Thomas, "Lost in the Storm: The Sociology of the Black Working Class, 1850–1990," *American Sociological Review* 65, no. 1 (2000): 128–137. Horton et al. refer to workers in poverty-level jobs as the bottom class. (I use the term poverty-level job or working poor here because the meaning is more clearly understood). First Horton and his colleagues determined the mean (23.9) and standard deviation (10.4) of the occupational income score (OCCSCORE) in 1950, using data from 1949 income. Then they determined the mean for ten broad occupational categories. (I replicated their analysis and collapsed farmers and farm laborers, as explained in chapter 2, and divided service workers into household and nonhousehold workers.) If the mean for a particular category was one standard deviation below the mean of OCCSCORE (13.5), those occupations were considered poverty-level jobs. For example, the mean for the category of service workers in private households was 6.0, hence domestic service was considered a poverty-level job.

25. Horton et al., "Lost in the Storm," 132.

26. Ibid., 133.

27. Jones, *Labor of Love*, 161.

28. Marks, "The Bone and Sinew of the Race," 165.

29. Jones, *Labor of Love*, 4.

30. Sojourner Truth, "Ain't I a Woman?" in *Let Nobody Turn Us Around: Voices of Resistance, Reform, and Renewal, An African American Anthology*, ed. Manning Marable and Leith Mullings (Lanham, Md.: Rowman & Littlefield, 2000), 67–68.

31. Aida Hurtado, "Relating to Privilege: Seduction and Rejection in the Subordination of White Women and Women of Color," *Signs* 14 (1989): 845.

32. Ibid.

33. Quoted in Landry, *Black Working Wives*, 56.

34. Ibid.

35. Ibid.

36. Hurtado, "Relating to Privilege," 845.

37. Landry, *Black Working Wives*, 58.

38. Glenn, "From Servitude to Service Work," 8.

39. Ibid., 14.

40. Katie G. Cannon, "The Emergence of a Black Feminist Consciousness," in *Feminist Interpretations of the Bible,* ed. Letty M. Russell (Philadelphia, Pa.: Westminster Press, 1985), 30.

41. See Jones, *Labor of Love,* 18.

42. Laurie B. Green, "'Where Would the Negro Women Apply for Work?': Gender, Race, and Labor in Wartime Memphis," *Labor: Studies in Working-Class History of the Americas* 3, no. 3 (2006): 98.

43. Ibid., 95.

44. Michael Keith Honey, *Black Workers Remember: An Oral History of Segregation, Unionism, and the Freedom Struggle* (Berkeley: University of California Press, 1999), 287.

45. Green, "Where Would the Negro Women Apply for Work?," 96.

46. Ibid.

47. Honey, *Black Workers Remember,* 287.

48. Green, "Where Would the Negro Women Apply for Work?," 97.

49. Barbara F. Reskin and Heidi I. Hartmann, *Women's Work, Men's Work: Sex Segregation on the Job* (Washington, D.C.: National Academy Press, 1986).

50. Asian men in the West performed reproductive labor as well; see Glenn, "From Servitude to Service Work."

51. Barbara Reskin, "Occupational Segregation by Race and Ethnicity among Women Workers," in *African-American and Latina Women at Work,* ed. Irene Browne (New York: Russell Sage Foundation, 1999), 183.

52. Manning Marable, *How Capitalism Underdeveloped Black America: Problems in Race, Political Economy, and Society* (London: Pluto Press, 2000), 70.

53. Frances Beale, "Double Jeopardy: To Be Black and Female," in *The Black Woman: An Anthology,* ed. Toni Cade (New York: Signet, 1970), 94.

54. Beverly Lindsay, "Minority Women in America: Black American, Native American, Chicana, and Asian American Women," in *The Study of Women: Enlarging Perspectives of Social Reality,* ed. Eloise C. Snyder (New York: Harper and Row, 1979), 324.

55. Deborah King, "Multiple Jeopardy, Multiple Consciousness: The Context of Black Feminist Ideology," *Signs* 14 (1988): 46.

56. Charisse Jones and Kumea Shorter-Gooden, *Shifting: The Double Lives of Black Women in America* (New York: Harper Perennial, 2003).

57. Marable, *How Capitalism Underdeveloped Black America,* 85.

CHAPTER 6. THE ILLUSION OF PROGRESS

1. E. Wilbur Bock, "Farmer's Daughter Effect: The Case of the Negro Female Professionals," *Phylon* (Spring 1969): 21.

2. Ibid.

3. Edward William Noland and Edward Wight Bakke, *Workers Wanted: A Study of Employers' Hiring Policies, Preferences and Practices in New Haven and Charlotte* (New York: Harper & Brothers, 1977), 65.

4. Ibid., 64.

5. Edward Gross, "Plus Ca Change . . . ? The Sexual Structure of Occupations over Time," *Social Problems* 16, no. 2 (1968): 198–208.

6. William T. Bielby and James N. Baron, "Men and Women at Work: Sex Segregation and Statistical Discrimination," *American Journal of Sociology* 91, no. 4 (1986): 759–799, quote at 760.

7. Mary C. King, "Occupational Segregation by Race and Sex, 1940–88," *Monthly Labor Review* 115, no. 4 (1992): 33.
8. The earnings of Black women compared to that of other groups in 1960 was computed from the real hourly wages reported by Cunningham and Zalokar. The average hourly wage estimate across occupations was as follows: Black women $2.87, White women $4.45, Black men $4.31, and White men $6.88. James S. Cunningham and Nadja Zalokar, "The Economic Progress of Black Women, 1940–1980: Occupational Distribution and Relative Wages," *Industrial and Labor Relations Review* 45, no. 3 (1992): 542.
9. In 1980, the hourly wage estimate was as follows: Black women $5.37 and White women $5.42 (ibid.).
10. In 1980, the hourly wage estimate was as follows: Black women $5.37, Black men $6.79, and White men $8.77 (ibid.).
11. In 1940, the hourly wage estimate was as follows: Black women $1.12, White women $2.54, Black men $1.80, and White men $3.79 (ibid.).
12. Francine D. Blau and Andrea H. Beller, "Black-White Earnings over the 1970s and 1980s: Gender Differences in Trends," *Review of Economics & Statistics* 74, no. 2 (1992): 285.
13. Ibid.
14. William J. Wilson, *The Declining Significance of Race: Blacks and Changing American Institutions* (Chicago: University of Chicago Press, 1980), 176–177.
15. A. Silvia Cancio, David T. Evans, and David Maume, Jr., "Reconsidering the Declining Significance of Race: Racial Differences in Early Career Wages," *American Sociological Review* 61, no. 4 (1996): 551.
16. Becky Pettit and Stephanie Ewert, "Employment Gains and Wage Declines: The Erosion of Black Women's Relative Wages since 1980," *Demography* 46, no. 3 (2009): 469.
17. Augustin Kwasi Fosu, "Occupational Gains of Black Women since the 1964 Civil Rights Act: Long-Term or Episodic?" *American Economic Review* 87, no. 2 (1997): 313.
18. King, "Occupational Segregation by Race and Sex, 1940–88," 34.
19. Noland and Bakke, *Workers Wanted*, 66.
20. Ibid., 32.
21. Ibid.
22. Ibid.
23. The provisions of Executive Order 11246 (Equal Employment Opportunity) of September 24, 1965, appear at 30 FR 12319, 12935, 3 CFR, 1964–1965 Comp., 339. Available at http://www.archives.gov/federal-register/codification/executive-order/11246.html.
24. Jonathan S. Leonard, "The Impact of Affirmative Action Regulation and Equal Employment Law on Black Employment," *Journal of Economic Perspectives* 4, no. 4 (1990): 49.
25. U.S. General Accounting Office, "The Equal Employment Opportunity Program for Federal Nonconstruction Contractors Can Be Improved," April 29, 1975, 30.
26. Leonard, "The Impact of Affirmative Action Regulation and Equal Employment Law on Black Employment," 49.
27. Ibid., 50.
28. Ibid., 53.
29. Ibid., 60.

30. Derrick Bell, Jr., "Foreword: Equal Employment Law and the Continuing Need for Self-Help," *Loyola University of Chicago Law Journal* 8 (1976–1977): 681.
31. Ibid.
32. See Augustin Kwasi Fosu, "Occupational Mobility of Black Women, 1958–1981: The Impact of Post-1964 Antidiscrimination Measures," *Industrial & Labor Relations Review* 45, no. 2 (1992): 281–294. See also Richard Freeman, "Changes in the Labor Market for Black Americans, 1948–72," *Brookings Papers on Economic Activity* 1 (1973): 118–119.
33. Leonard, "The Impact of Affirmative Action Regulation and Equal Employment Law on Black Employment," 50.
34. Kevin Stainback and Donald Tomaskovic-Devey, "Intersections of Power and Privilege: Long-Term Trends in Managerial Representation," *American Sociological Review* 74 (2009): 800–820.
35. Cunningham and Zalokar, "The Economic Progress of Black Women, 1940–1980," 542.
36. Ibid.
37. Mary C. King, "Black Women's Breakthrough into Clerical Work: An Occupational Tipping Model," *Journal of Economic Issues* 27, no. 4 (1993): 1097–1124.
38. Ibid., 1107.
39. Kevin Stainback, Corre L. Robinson, and Donald Tomaskovic-Devey, "Race and Workplace Integration: A Politically Mediated Process?" *American Behavioral Scientist* 48, no. 9 (2005): 1200.
40. For further discussion, see Donald Tomaskovic-Devey, Catherine Zimmer, Kevin Stainback, Corre Robinson, Tiffany Taylor, and Tricia McTague, "Documenting Desegregation: Segregation in American Workplaces by Race, Ethnicity, and Sex, 1966–2003," *American Sociological Review* 71, no. 4 (2006): 565–588.
41. Leonard, "The Impact of Affirmative Action Regulation and Equal Employment Law on Black Employment," 58.
42. Evan Thomas, Carolyn Lesh, and Melissa Ludtke, "Assault on Affirmative Action," *Time*, February 25, 1985, http://www.time.com/time/magazine/article/0,9171,961192-2,00.html#ixzz0mWIrCgbW.
43. Ibid.
44. Cancio, Evans, and Maume, "Reconsidering the Declining Significance of Race," 548.
45. Ibid., 553.
46. Ibid., 542.
47. For further discussion, see Lori G. Kletzer, "Job Displacement, 1979–86: How Blacks Fared Relative to Whites," *Monthly Labor Review* 114, no. 7 (1991): 17–25.
48. For further discussion of this, see Arne L. Kalleberg, Barbara F. Reskin, and Ken Hudson, "Bad Jobs in America: Standard and Nonstandard Employment Relations and Job Quality in the United States," *American Sociological Review* 65 (2000): 256–278.
49. Pettit and Ewert, "Employment Gains and Wage Declines," 474.
50. For further discussion of this, see John Bound and Richard B. Freeman, "What Went Wrong? The Erosion of Relative Earnings and Employment among Young Black Men in the 1980s," *Quarterly Journal of Economics* 107

(1991): 201–232. See also Katherine Newman, *No Shame in My Game: The Working Poor in the Inner City* (New York: Vintage, 2000).

51. Roberta Spalter-Roth and Cynthia Deitch, "'I Don't Feel Right Sized; I Feel Out-of-Work Sized': Gender, Race, Ethnicity, and the Unequal Costs of Displacement," *Work and Occupations* 26, no. 4 (1999): 449.

52. Sharon Collins, *Black Corporate Executives* (Philadelphia, Pa.: Temple University Press, 1997).

53. Lynn C. Burbridge, "The Reliance of African-American Women on Government and Third-Sector Employment," *American Economic Review* 84, no. 2 (1994): 104.

54. Ibid., 105.

55. King, "Occupational Segregation by Race and Sex," 34.

56. Lynn C. Burbridge, "The Occupational Structure of Non-Profit Industries: Implications for Women," in *Women and Power in the Nonprofit Sector*, ed. Teresa Odendahl and Michael O'Neill (San Francisco: Jossey-Bass, 1994), 121–154.

57. Yvonne D. Newsome and F. Nii-Amoo Dodoo, "Reversal of Fortune: Explaining the Decline in Black Women's Earnings," *Gender and Society* 16, no. 4 (2002): 453.

58. John Bound and Laura Dresser, "Losing Ground: The Erosion of the Relative Earnings of African American Women during the 1980s," in *Latinas and African-American Women at Work*, ed. Irene Browne (New York: Russell Sage Foundation, 1999), 60–104.

59. Pettit and Ewert, "Employment Gains and Wage Declines," 473.

60. Scott Cummings, "Vulnerability to the Effects of Recession: Minority and Female Workers," *Social Forces* 65, no. 3 (1987): 834–857.

61. Pettit and Ewert, "Employment Gains and Wage Declines," 487.

62. Ibid., 487–489. Also see Newsome and Dodoo, "Reversal of Fortune," 451; and Irene Browne, "Explaining the Black-White Gap in Labor Force Participation among Women Heading Households," *American Sociological Review* 62 (1997): 236–252.

63. See F. Noo-Amoo Dodoo and Patricia Kasari, "Race and Female Occupational Location in America," *Journal of Black Studies* 25, no. 4 (1995): 465–474. See also Pettit and Ewert, "Employment Gains and Wage Declines."

64. Newsome and Dodoo, "Reversal of Fortune," 451.

65. Ibid., 461.

66. Irene Browne, Cynthia Hewitt, Leann Tigges, and Gary Green, "Why Does Job Segregation Lead to Wage Inequality among African Americans? Person, Place, Sector, or Skills," *Social Science Research* 30, no. 3 (2001): 473.

67. Julianne Malveaux, "Low-Wage Black Women: Occupational Descriptions, Strategies for Change," unpublished paper prepared for the NAACP Legal Defense and Educational Fund, Inc., 1984, cited in King, "Black Women's Breakthrough into Clerical Work," 1098.

68. King, "Black Women's Breakthrough into Clerical Work," 1106.

69. Evelyn Nakano Glenn and Charles M. Tolbert, II, "Technology and Emerging Patterns of Stratification for Women of Color: Race and Gender Segregation in Computer Occupations," in *Women, Work and Technology: Transformations*, ed. Barbara Drygulski Wright (Ann Arbor: University of Michigan Press, 1987), 318–331.

70. Lynn C. Burbridge, "The Labor Market for Home Care Workers: Demand, Supply, and Institutional Barriers," *Gerontologist* 3, no. 1 (1993): 41–46.

71. Ryan A. Smith, "Race, Gender, and Authority in the Workplace: Theory and Research," *Annual Review of Sociology* 28, no. 1 (2002): 535.

72. Stainback and Tomaskovic-Devey, "Intersections of Power and Privilege," 810–813.

73. Ibid., 808–809.

74. Income is based on occupation and is thus a key determinant of economic class. This argument is disputed by scholars with a Marxist orientation because of its departure from arguments based on the relationship of the worker to the means of production, which is the central contention of Karl Marx's conceptualization of class. See Erik Olin Wright, "Class and Occupation," *Theory and Society* 9, no. 1 (1980): 177. However, Marx's criterion for class identification as whether a man "is an employer who has the capital to buy the labor of others or an employee who sells his labor" is no longer feasible because of the existence of large capitalistic enterprises where even the controlling managers are employees of the corporation; see Peter M. Blau and Otis D. Duncan, *The American Occupational Structure* (New York: John Wiley & Sons, 1967), 6. I take a feminist historical materialist approach to class, which focuses on structural change in the economy.

75. Robert L. Kaufman, "Assessing Alternative Perspectives on Race and Sex Employment Segregation," *American Sociological Review* 67, no. 4 (2002): 550.

76. Ibid.

77. Ibid., 565.

78. Ibid.

79. Patricia Hill Collins, "Toward a New Vision: Race, Class, and Gender as Categories of Analysis and Connection," *Race, Sex & Class* 1 (1993): 25–45. Also see Bonnie Thornton Dill and Ruth Enid Zambrana, eds., *Emerging Intersections: Race, Class, and Gender in Theory, Policy, and Practice* (New Brunswick, N.J.: Rutgers University Press, 2009).

80. Ivy Ken, "Beyond the Intersection: A New Culinary Metaphor for Race-Class-Gender Studies," *Sociological Theory* 26, no. 2 (2008): 162.

81. Julie Kmec, "Minority Job Concentration and Wages," *Social Problems* 50, no 1 (2003): 41.

82. Joan Acker, *Class Questions: Feminist Answers* (Lanham, Md.: Rowman & Littlefield, 2006), 11.

83. Ibid., 7.

84. Mary Church Terrell, "The Progress of Colored Women," in *Let Nobody Turn Us Around: Voices of Resistance, Reform, and Renewal, An African American Anthology*, ed. Manning Marable and Leith Mullings (Lanham, Md.: Rowman & Littlefield, 2000), 176.

Index

Acker, Joan, 152

affirmative action, 137–139, 141–143

Agnew, Samuel (planter), 37

agricultural labor. *See* farm labor

"Ain't I a Woman?" (speech), 119

Alexander, Sadie Tanner Mossell, 110–111

All of the Women Are White, All Blacks Are Men, But Some of Us Are Brave (Hull et al.), 12

Amalgamated Meat Cutters and Butcher Workmen of North America, 82

American Work (Jones), 98

Anderson, Karen Tucker, 91, 92, 102

Anderson, Mary, 68

Atlanta, Ga., 60, 110; Atlanta City Council, 60

authority in the workplace, 147–150

autonomy, 37–39, 40–41. *See also* emancipation; post-emancipation era

Bakke, Edward Wight, 109, 131–132, 136, 137

Baldwin, James, 8

Barbee, Annie (tobacco factory worker), 78–79

Barnwell, Hagar (former slave), 35

Baron, James, 133

Bates, Evelyn (factory worker), 95

Beale, Frances, 22, 125

Bell, Derrick Jr., 138

Beller, Andrea H., 135

Bielby, William, 133

Black Codes, 32, 48

Black Feminist Thought (Collins), 12

Black men, 5, 101, 104–105, 112–113, 122–126; farm labor and, 103–104; industrial work and, 22, 74–75

Blacks' labor, 31–33, 72

Black Wealth / White Wealth (Oliver and Shapiro), 97

Blackwelder, Julia Kirk, 63, 110

Black women: scholarship and, 11–13; as servile, 54–55, 65, 69, 118

Blau, Francine D., 135

Blau, Peter, 25

Blauner, Robert, 23, 30

Bock, E. Wilbur, 130

Bonilla-Silva, Eduardo, 97

Bound, John, 144

Branch, Irene (factory worker), 94–95

Branch, Rosetta (tobacco factory worker), 79

Browne, Irene, 14, 145

Brown v. Board of Education (1954), 95

Burbridge, Lynn C., 144

Callis, Myra Colson, 65–66

Cancio, A. Silvia, 142, 143

Cannon, Katie, 122

capitalism, 124–125

census, 42–43, 50, 163n2 (intro.), 171–172n2

Cheatham, Pansy (tobacco factory worker), 78

Chicago Federation of Labor, 83

Circular 13, 38–39

Circular 15, 39

Civil Rights Act (1964), 1, 14, 136–139, 141. *See also* post–civil rights era

Clark, Elias (freedman), 40

class, 6–7, 13, 111, 124–125, 150–153, 181n74; domestic service and, 68, 171n51. *See also* poverty

Class Questions (Acker), 152

Clayton, Horace, 63

clerical work, 17, 22, 57, 103, 110–111, 129; employer preferences and, 109, 131–132; growth of, 5, 102, 140–141; in post–civil rights era, 127–128, 131–133, 140–141, 145–147; poverty and, 147–148; White women in, 106, 107–108, 112

coercion, 35, 60

Collins, Patricia Hill, 12, 151

Connell, R. W., 97

contracts, 39–40

cooks, 52, 65–66

cotton mills, 76

coverture, 39

craftsmen, 71–74, 102, 105, 129, 171n1

credit system, 41–42

Cunningham, James S., 63, 178n8

Darity, William, 25

Davis, Adrienne, 26–27

defense jobs, 64, 123

democracy, 28

desegregation, 77, 95–96, 141–142. *See also* post–civil rights era

desirable occupations, 103, 110–111, 129, 171–172n2. *See also* undesirable work

devalued occupations, 1, 8, 22, 69–70, 121–122, 152. *See also* undesirable work

dirty work, 4, 87–88, 89–90, 96, 117–118, 129. *See also* undesirable work

disadvantage, 98, 122, 151, 152. *See also* labor market disadvantage; oppression

discrimination, 1, 6–7, 14, 24–25, 91, 95; Civil Rights Act and, 136; domestic service and, 63–64; wages and, 145. *See also* employer preferences; segregation

dissimilarity indexes, 133

division of labor, 9–10, 10–11, 28, 72–75. *See also* segregation

Dodoo, F. Nii-Amoo, 144

domesticity, 33–34, 99

domestic service, 1, 3, 4, 49–70, 105–106, 129; Black men and, 22, 122; as Black women's work, 49–51, 57–64, 117–118, 132–133; class and, 68, 171n51; decline of, 17, 102; as devalued, 69–70; employers and, 52–55, 60; factory work and, 90–91; immigration and, 53, 57–59; men and, 49, 169n2; proportions of workers in, 50, 56, 58, 59; race and, 51–55; in Washington, D.C., 65–69; White women and, 22, 55, 57–59; womanhood and, 120–121

Dove, Mary (tobacco factory worker), 78

Drake, St. Clair, 63

Dred Scott v. Sandford (1857), 27

Dresser, Laura, 144

Du Bois, W.E.B., 8, 85

Dudden, Faye, 52

Duncan, Otis, 25

economic growth, 6, 17, 139–140, 141

education, 4, 63, 109–112, 143–144, 145, 153

Ellis, Elaine, 46

emancipation, 3, 29–30, 113–114. *See also* post-emancipation era employer neutrality, 93

employer preferences, 14–15, 23–25,
65–66, 91–92, 150–151, 165n36;
clerical work and, 109, 131–132;
manual labor and, 91, 102;
occupational opportunities and,
109–110; stereotypes of Blacks and,
136–137

employers, 5, 6–7, 70, 91, 142;
affirmative action and, 138;
domestic service and, 52–55, 60;
integration and, 77; in meatpacking
industry, 86–87. *See also* planters

*The Employment of Negroes in the
District of Columbia* (study), 65

Epstein, Cynthia Fuchs, 9

Equal Employment Opportunity
Commission, 142–143

Erwin, W. A. (mill owner), 77

Evans, David T., 142, 143

Ewert, Stephanie, 135, 143, 145

Executive Order 11246, 137

factory overseers, 75

factory work. *See* industrial work

farmers, 42–43, 104

farm labor, 1, 3, 4, 26–48; Black men
in, 103–104, 122; Black women
and, 42–48, 102, 117–118, 129;
decline of, 17, 45–46, 102, 117;
defined, 42–43; emancipation
and, 31–42; poverty and, 118;
sharecropping, 41–42, 42–43, 48;
slavery and, 26–30, 47. *See also*
plantation labor; planters

farm laborers, 42, 104, 105

farm owners, 42–43

federal contractors, 138, 142

femininity. *See* womanhood

feminized occupations, 9, 108–109,
111–112, 131. *See also* women's
work

Firestone Tire Company, 94, 95

Foner, Eric, 31, 32, 36–37, 38, 39, 40

Fosu, Augustin Kwasi, 135, 139

Frederickson, George, 29

Freedmen's Bureau, 4, 32–33, 34–35,
37, 39, 40

freedom, 37–39, 40–41, 42. *See also*
emancipation; post-emancipation
era

free labor, 31–33, 34–36, 37, 47

Freeman, Richard, 139

gender, 1, 5, 12–13, 100, 107, 163n2
(intro.); class and, 150–153; clerical
work and, 17, 22, 103; factory work
and, 74–75; intersectional theory
and, 97–98; poverty-level jobs and,
114–116; race and, 2–3, 121–126.
See also Black men; Black women;
intersectional theory; men's work;
White men; White women;
women's work

General Cable Corporation, 95

German women, 54

girls for "general house-work," 52–53

Glenn, Evelyn Nakano, 10, 42, 43,
52, 120, 147

Gordon, Lula (Black woman worker),
62

government work, 144

Great Migration, 44–45, 60

Green, Gary, 145

Green, Laurie B., 63, 124

Greig, Ruth B., 69

Gross, Edward, 133

Hammond, Sen. James Henry (D-
S.C.), 29

Herbst, Alma, 85

Hewitt, Cynthia, 145

hiring practices, 52, 142

hiring preferences. *See* employer
preferences

"Hoe Emma Hoe" (song), 43–44

hooks, bell, 11
Horton, James Oliver, 28
House and Senate Committees on Labor and Public Welfare, 137
household service. *See* domestic service
Housewives' League of Richmond, 61
Howard, Oliver Otis, 37, 38–39
Hunter, Addie W., 109
Hurtado, Aida, 11, 119

ideology of separate spheres, 99–100
immigration, 6, 53, 57–59, 80–81, 88
income. *See* wages
income inequality, 15–21, 142–143, 144–145, 149
The Independent (magazine), 120
industrialization, 71, 99–100, 117. *See also* industrial work
industrial work, 1, 3, 5, 6, 22, 71–96, 171n1; benefits of, 71; Black men and, 22, 74–75; Black women's exclusion from, 72–75; decline of, 143; Irish immigrants and, 80–81; in meatpacking industry, 85–88; in the North, 80–85; in the South, 76–79; World War I and, 88–91; World War II and, 91–95. *See also* craftsmen; operatives
interracial cooperation, 83–84
intersectional theory, 2–3, 8–25, 121–126, 150–153; income inequality and, 19–21; labor market disadvantage and, 14–25; occupational opportunity and, 3–4, 97–98, 113, 116; privilege/oppression and, 9–13
Irish immigrants, 53, 80–81

Janiewski, Dolores, 79
job growth, 140
job security, 143–144

Johnson, Andrew, 38–39
Johnson, Lyndon B., 137
Jones, Jacqueline, 31, 98, 117, 118; on domestic servants, 62; on employer preferences, 92; on factories, 93; on farm labor, 46; on freedom, 35, 42; on wage equality, 11

Kaufman, Robert L., 151
Ken, Ivy, 151
Kerber, Linda, 32
King, Deborah, 125
King, Martin Luther, 123
King, Mary C., 133–134, 136, 140, 144

labor contract system, 39–40
laborers, 74, 105, 171n1. *See also* industrial work
labor market, 71, 97, 124
labor market disadvantage, 14–25; causes of, 14–15; intersectional theory and, 21–25; quantifiability of, 15–20
labor queues, 23–24, 99, 151, 153
labor shortages, 1, 17, 24, 40, 140; domestic service and, 53, 69–70; in wartime, 64, 91
labor system, U.S., 31, 116–117
land, 36, 38–39
Landry, Bart, 111, 120
Langhorne, Orra, 55
laundry work, 10, 65–66, 66–68, 117, 164n8
Lawson, the Rev. James, 123–124
Leonard, Jonathan S., 137, 138, 139, 142
Lieberson, Stanley, 23, 84, 99
Lincoln, Abraham, 30, 37
Lindsay, Beverly, 125
Local 651 (meatpackers' union), 83–84
Lorber, Judith, 13

Mackay, Charles, 51
Malveaux, Julieanne, 146
managerial occupations, 5, 110–111, 112, 129, 133, 139, 148–149
manhood, 123. *See also* womanhood
manual labor, 91, 102
Marable, Manning, 124, 125
Marks, Carole, 118
marriage, 57, 99, 111, 145
Mason, Patrick, 25
maternalism/paternalism, 69, 123–124
Maume, David Jr., 142, 143
McGhee, Hazel (laundry worker), 123
meatpacking industry, 81–88
mechanization, 78, 95. *See also* factory work; industrialization
men's work, 89–90, 102, 112–113, 131; farm labor as, 26–27, 33, 44, 118; industrial work as, 86, 96. *See also* women's work
Misra, Joya, 14
Montgomery Ward, 109
Myrdal, Gunnar, 98–99

New Orleans, La., 110
Newsome, Yvonne D., 144
New York Times, 52–53, 53–54
Noland, Edward William, 109, 131–132, 136, 137
nonhousehold service occupations, 22, 100, 102, 106, 129; distribution of workers in, 149; poverty and, 147–148, 150; proportion of Black women in, 127, 146–147

occupational categories, 42–43, 101, 102, 103, 118, 127–131, 176n24. *See also* clerical work; domestic service; farm labor; household service; industrial work; nonhousehold service; occupational distribution

occupational distribution, 2, 100, 104, 107, 134, 149–151. *See also* occupational categories
occupational income score, 15–20, 164–165n23, 176n24
occupational mobility, 4, 135–136, 140, 141
occupational opportunities, 5, 14, 97–126; access to, 15–20, 22, 126; Black men and, 112–113, 122–126; clerical work and, 102–103, 106, 107–109; education and, 109, 110–112; farm labor and, 102, 103–104, 117–118; gender segregation and, 98–101, 110–113, 122, 124–126; industrial work and, 105, 106; intersectional theory and, 3–4, 97–98, 113, 116; poverty and, 113–116; racial ideology and, 116–121; racial segregation and, 98, 101–107, 110–113, 121–122; sales occupations and, 109–110; service occupations and, 99–100, 105–106, 117–118, 120–121; structure of, 3, 8, 112, 115–116, 121–122, 127
O'Leary, Elizabeth, 61
Oliver, Melvin, 97
operatives, 5, 71–76, 102, 105–106, 129, 130, 133
oppression, 9, 10, 13, 14, 97, 124–125, 151. *See also* discrimination; segregation
overseers, 75

Parrish, John (planter), 36
Pettit, Becky, 135, 143, 145
plantation labor, 32–42; Black Codes and, 32; free labor and, 33, 34–36; labor contract system and, 39–40; sharecropping and, 41–42. *See also* farm labor

planters, 32–42; Black women and, 34–35, 40–41; command of labor and, 36–37; Freedmen's Bureau and, 32–33, 37–39

post–civil rights era, 5–6, 127–153; affirmative action and, 137–139, 141–143; class and, 150–153; economy and, 139–141, 143–144, 145; employer discrimination and, 136–138, 150–151; occupational distribution of Black women and, 127–134, 143–147, 149; wages and, 134–136, 142–143, 145, 147–148, 149–150

post–emancipation era, 4, 31–42, 113–114; farm labor and, 34–36; free labor and, 31–33, 37–38; labor contracts and, 39–40; land and, 38–39; planters and, 32–42; sharecropping and, 41–42

poverty, 6–7, 113–116; clerical workers and, 147–148; industrial workers and, 73–74; nonhousehold service work and, 147–148, 150. *See also* class

poverty-level jobs, 113–116, 176n24

Price, Gwilym A., 92–93

private sector, 144

privilege, 2, 98, 122, 151; labor market and, 22–25, 97, 124; men and, 22, 126; oppression and, 8–13

productive labor, 9, 27. *See also* reproductive labor

professional jobs, 22, 106, 110–111, 112, 129; increase of, 5, 17; as women's work, 130

progress, 5–6; economic growth and, 139–140; lack of post-1980, 141–150. *See also* post–civil rights era

"The Progress of Colored Women" (speech) (1904), 8, 152

public sector, 144

queuing theory, 23, 151. *See also* labor queues

race, 1, 2–3, 5, 12–13, 22, 150–153; census data on, 163n2 (intro.); domestic service and, 51–55; factory work and, 74–75; intersectional theory and, 97–98, 121–126; occupational distribution and, 107; poverty-level jobs and, 114–116; social mobility and, 59; womanhood and, 119–121. *See also* Black men; Black women; intersectional theory; racism; White men; White women

racial ideology, 27–30, 65, 79, 80–81, 98, 118–121

Racial Oppression in America (Blauner), 30

racism, 8, 11–12, 29–30, 97, 121–126. *See also* discrimination; intersectional theory; race; racial ideology

Reagan, Ronald, 6, 142

reproductive labor, 9, 10, 27–28, 124

reserve labor pool, 88–89, 121–122

Reskin, Barbara, 24, 165n36

Retail Merchants' Association of Richmond, 61

Roberts, Dorothy, 27

Robinson, Corre L., 141–142

Roediger, David, 80

Rollins, Judith, 59

Roos, Patricia, 24, 165n36

Roosevelt, Franklin D., 62

Sager, C. Douglas (employer), 66–68

salaries. *See* wages

sales work, 5, 22, 57, 102, 109–112, 129

San Antonio, Tex., 110

Scales, Anderson (sharecropper), 41

Scott, Blanche (tobacco factory worker), 77–78
Sealy, Angeline (field hand), 35
seasonal laborers, 42
segregation, occupational, 110–113, 121–122, 124–126, 136, 153; employers and, 25, 136, 150–151; gender and, 130–131, 133–134; in industrial work, 76–77, 79, 86; in private sector, 144; undesirable work and, 98–101, 101–107, 129, 132–133; wages and, 113, 145, 147. *See also* desegregation; segregation, physical
segregation, physical, 5, 76–77, 79, 86, 92–93. *See also* desegregation; segregation, occupational
the servant problem, 53–54
service economy, 6, 143
service occupations, 99–100, 117, 127. *See also* domestic service; nonhousehold service occupations
servile, Black women as, 54–55, 65, 69, 79, 118
sexism, 8, 11–12, 124–125, 125–126. *See also* gender; intersectional theory
Shapiro, Thomas, 97
sharecropping, 41–42, 42–43, 48
Sherman, William T., 38
Sims, Altha (Black woman worker), 63–64
skilled laborers, 71–74, 171n1
skilled work, 105, 122
slavery, 4, 26–30, 47, 120. *See also* emancipation; post-emancipation era
Smith, Clarence (Black male worker), 123
social mobility, 59
Southern Presbyterian Review, 39–40
Special Field Order No. 15 (1865), 38

Stainback, Kevin, 139, 141–142, 148
Stockyards Labor Council (SLC), 83–84
strikebreakers, 81–82, 85
strikes, 92, 123
Swift and Company, 83

teaching, 130
tenant farmers, 42
Terrell, Mary Church, 8, 152
textile mills, 77
Thurow, Lester, 23
Tigges, Leann, 145
Tilly, Charles, 23
Title VII (of Civil Rights Act), 136, 138
tobacco factories, 76, 77–79
Tolbert, Charles M., II, 147
Tomaskovic-Devey, Donald, 139, 141–142, 148
Truth, Sojourner, 119

undesirable work, 5, 15, 47, 79, 85, 98–107; census data and, 171–172n2; devalued occupations, 1, 8, 22, 69–70, 121–122, 152; dirty work, 4, 87–88, 89–90, 96, 117–118, 129; segregation by gender and, 98–101; segregation by race and, 98, 101–107, 132–133
unemployment, 144–145
unions, 80–85, 90, 94–95
unskilled laborers, 71–74, 85, 99
unskilled work, 80–81, 105
"upstairs girls," 52
U.S. General Accounting Office, 137

vagrancy laws, 32, 39, 48
Vickers, Milton, 142
violence, 35, 48

wages, 6, 10–11, 40, 139, 178n8, 181n74; for domestic servants, 68–69; inequality of, 15–21, 142–143, 144–145, 149; post-1960, 134–136. *See also* poverty
Washington, D.C., 65–69
Washington, Mary Helen (Black woman worker), 57
Watson plantation, 34, 36
Westinghouse Electric Corporation, 93, 95
White, Deborah Gray, 31, 35
White men, 5, 18–20, 74–75, 101, 103–105, 131
White privilege, 2, 22, 126
White women, 5, 10, 11–12, 90, 102, 105–107, 129; in clerical work, 106, 107–108, 112; in domestic service, 22, 55, 57–59; roles of in factories, 74–75; womanhood and, 4, 34, 120
Wilson, Francille Rusan, 111
Wilson, William Julius, 135
Winchester Repeating Arms Company, 93

womanhood, 4, 26–27, 34, 47–48, 119–121, 126. *See also* manhood
women, 11, 99–100, 100–101. *See also* Black women; gender; White women
Women's Bureau of the U.S. Department of Labor, 68
Women's Rights Convention (1851), 119
women's work, 9, 26, 33, 130, 153, 164n8; domestic service as, 4, 49, 118; expansion of, 22, 117; racial typing of, 110, 122. *See also* feminized occupations; men's work
Woodson, Doris Walker, 63
working conditions, 77–79, 85–86
work or fight laws, 61
Works Progress Administration (WPA), 61–62
World War I, 60–61, 88–91
World War II, 17, 63–64, 91–95, 123

Zalokar, Nadja, 63, 178n8

About the Author

ENOBONG HANNAH BRANCH is an assistant professor at the University of Massachusetts–Amherst. She received her Ph.D. in sociology from the State University of New York at Albany (2007) and her B.S. in biology from Howard University (2002). Her areas of specialty are race, racism, and inequality; intersectional theory (race, gender, and class); work and occupations; historical demography; and evaluation and applied research. Her research focus lies primarily in the study of Blacks contemporarily and historically. Dr. Branch is interested in the heterogeneity of the Black experience created by the intersection of gender, nationality, citizenship, and economic class as well as the sociohistorical context.

CPSIA information can be obtained at www.ICGtesting.com
Printed in the USA
LVOW081515140312

273092LV00001B/5/P